THE COMPLETE GUIDE TO WRITING FOR YOUNG ADULTS

VOLUME I

Edited by Gabrielle Harbowy

THE COMPLETE GUIDE TO WRITING FOR YOUNG ADULTS

VOLUME I

DRAGON
MOON
PRESS

Acknowledgments

Many thanks to Gwen Gades and Dragon Moon Press; to our fantastic contributors for their insight, time, and patience; and to Grace Darling, production assistant.

CONTENTS

For Patricia Dobson —
who made the library at
Boyd H. Anderson High School
my home away from home.

FOREWORD

When you browse the bookstore shelves and pull down a writing guide, you generally see the same predictable chapter headings. There's a chapter on plotting, maybe one on building suspense. A chapter on writing dialogue, a chapter on humor, a chapter on worldbuilding, a chapter on grammar, a chapter on editing, and at the back there's a list of markets (which was already out of date before the book even went to print).

When I was offered the chance to create this book, I knew I wanted to take a different approach. I didn't want the same generic topics, I wanted to handle topics specific to writing for young adults. All genres of Young Adult, not just science fiction and fantasy. To that end, I've assembled a star-studded team of authors and industry pros for you and asked them questions that emerging authors don't usually get a chance to ask.

In these pages, you will find the difference between YA and Middle Grade; the difference between YA and adult fiction that happens to have a young adult as a main character. Ever wonder why is it important to get the grown-ups out of the way in order for adventure to happen? Some of these chapters may contradict each other; this doesn't mean anyone is in error, it's an indication of the difference between theory and practice, and how widely definitions can vary in the real world of publishing, where rules are a bit less hard-and-fast. Take that and learn from it, too.

Do readers automatically side with a character and form teams, or does the writer deliberately create the environment that encourages such loyalty? How much science is appropriate for a YA novel? How can you help to push back against gender stereotypes in young adult fiction, and how can you write an authentic-feeling transgendered character for a young adult audience? What happens when you live in a community that isn't friendly to the kinds of stories you write? How has book blogging revolutionized social media for YA writers and readers? What can an agent really do for you? What's it like to try to make a living out of collaborating with your BFF? And, are authors responsible for limiting their content and only telling stories that teach life lessons?

So...pull up a seat under the dragon's wing, get comfortable, and let's tell some stories.

Gabrielle Harbowy
San Francisco, CA—August 5, 2014

CHAPTER 1

The Emergence of YA

Adrienne Kress

It's truly exciting how popular fiction for young people has become over the last decade. As a market, it is now quite clearly a force to be reckoned with. In these more difficult economic times, it is one of the few categories, along with Adult Romance, to have actually seen an increase in sales rather than a decline. But with popularity come scrutiny and judgment. And such scrutiny and judgment are only magnified when it comes to work aimed at young people.

Articles are written about how much darker YA is now compared with how it used to be. Concerned parents/teachers/ others discuss how much sex and violence they see in it now. "What has happened to YA?" many moan.

My answer: Nothing. Nothing has happened to YA. Because until recently, YA didn't exist.

Not so, not so, others retort, what about…Judy Blume! Judy Blume, the literary patron saint of young people, and my personal literary obsession during those formative years. How could one forget about Judy? But Judy Blume does not write what you think she writes.

Let me explain.

My argument has been, and continues to be, that the YA of my youth, of the youth of anyone born before 1980 or so, is not the YA of today. The YA of yesteryear was, in fact, are you ready for it…MG, aka Middle Grade, aka books for 8- to 12-year-olds.

Here's where things get delightfully confusing. It all comes down to words. Words, words, words. We assign books to categories. We give them names to make life just that much better organized. To impose some semblance of sanity on a chaotic world. Deep stuff. And so it was, once upon a time, that books which were intended for younger people several decades ago were called Young Adult. These books were not read by teens. At least, most of them were not. (There are, of course, exceptions to everything, but bear with me for a minute.) These books were read by what we now call tweens: kids 8 to 12. Not only do we know this by chatting with our friends and finding out what they were reading at certain ages, we can also determine it by looking at the usual ages portrayed in some of the most popular Young Adult books from back then. Margaret in *Are You There God? It's Me Margaret* is 11. There is simply no way that, as teenagers, we were reading books about kids younger than we were.

What were we oh so grown up teens reading then? We were reading adult books. In my day (imagine me saying that while sitting on a sun-bleached rocking chair on my front porch) we were cutting their teeth on Grisham and Anne Rice. We were also studying Shakespeare from our very first year of high school. Aside from the fact that our reading comprehension was at a level which meant we could appreciate and understand adult books, teens—and we've all been there—like to get to adulthood as quickly as possible. To quote C. S. Lewis:

> "To be concerned about being grown up, to admire the grown up because it is grown up, to blush at the suspicion of being childish; these things are the marks of childhood and adolescence."—*On Three Ways of Writing for Children* (1952)

So, the idea of reading books where the character might even be the same age, let alone younger, was hardly something teens were interested in. It also didn't help that many teens had already gone through the growing pains which those supposed Young Adult books addressed. We weren't getting the opportunity to read about our own specific life issues, but were rather experiencing a walk down memory lane.

This was our relatively recent reading past.

Then, two things happened.

First: *Harry Potter* was published and became a worldwide phenomenon for readers of all ages. Before *Harry Potter*, children's literature was certainly not considered a category of fiction in which blockbusters could be created. Suddenly, publishers discovered that there was money to be made there. But what was also interesting about *Harry Potter* when it comes to its influence on the future Young Adult category was not just the massive impact it made on the publishing scene, but how the Potter books themselves grew up. I'd argue the first three books fall into the MG category, but the books from four onwards are centered very much around being a teenager. When readers start as tweens but age along with the characters, you wind up with teenagers actually reading books with teenagers as the main characters. It's almost like *Harry Potter* tricked teens into wanting to read about themselves and not about adults.

The second thing that happened was *Twilight*. It happened along on the tails of *Harry Potter*, just when the teens finishing *Harry Potter* and hungry for something new to consume. Here was a book where the primary story was a romance; there is very little plot aside from two characters falling in love in the first novel. And this was actually quite important, because it showed that teens were absolutely happy to consume fiction that reflected back to them their emotional angst and concerns. The first book is about the teen girl's fear of being an outsider, the overwhelming feeling of that first real love, and some school politics thrown into the mix. It showed that teens had the same kind of romantic angst as adults (and the adult romance market is the most profitable adult market), and most importantly, it doesn't talk down to them. It's a romance novel that just happens to be about teens.

This meant that for the first time since *Harry Potter*, teens were reading books with teen characters. Books about teens were actually being read by teens.

And so the term Young Adult was redefined. It no longer belonged to the tween Judy Blume set. It belonged to teenagers. The tween set was defined as either Middle Grade or simply "Ages 8 to 12." And thus a new category was born.

But not everyone understood that. Many people who grew up with the old definition of Young Adult describing the books we read as tweens started to see the new Young Adult taking off. They noticed that the new Young Adult books were sexier and darker than the tween Young Adult novels of their youth. They noticed these books also dealt with some pretty dark issues, and many people freaked out. Meghan Cox Gurdon of the *Wall Street Journal* described YA in an article that was a "call to arms" to end the darkness:

"Pathologies that went undescribed in print 40 years ago, that were still only sparingly outlined a generation ago, are now spelled out in stomach-clenching detail. Profanity that would get a song or movie branded with a parental warning is, in young-adult novels, so commonplace that most reviewers do not even remark upon it."

A general cry of "Won't someone think of the children?" went out, and adults began debating what teens ought to be reading. They didn't stop to consider who the real readership of Young Adult was now. And even if they did, they seemed to forget what teens had been reading for generations—that these were the same teens who read adult books in high school; the same teens who read Shakespeare (which, lest we forget, is rife with sex and violence). They were comparing the Young Adult books of the past—the ones we now call Middle Grade—with the Young Adult novels of the present. Comparing books that are aimed at completely different audiences, and then condemning them.

But this was a false comparison.

Young Adult is no longer Middle Grade.

Young Adult is Young Adult.

What Is MG?

MG stands for middle grade. It is the category of fiction aimed for 8-to-12-year-olds. In other words, novels in this category are aimed at kids turning into pre-teens. MG is not picture books, nor Chapter books. MG is for readers who have a good, solid grasp on language, though still obviously have much to learn. It is for kids who want to read a book that is a book. These novels are what many consider classic children's lit. The kind of novels parents read to their kids before bed, or teachers read to a group of kids sitting on the floor in front of them. These are the novels Disney has made into classic animated films. *Peter Pan. Alice in Wonderland.* The first three Harry Potters. These are all middle grade novels.

Within these books, you will find certain repeating elements. The characters in these books tend to be on the older spectrum of the MG range. Harry Potter turns 11 in the first book. Wendy from *Peter Pan* is on the cusp of becoming a teenager. Percy Jackson is twelve. Margaret from *Are You There God? It's Me Margaret* is in grade six. It is rare that the main character of an MG is any older than thirteen unless he/she is in a more contemporary series where the main character has grown older in subsequent books.

Thematically, these novels deal with growing up. The lessons in these books can range from more specific (e.g. *Iggy's House* by Judy Blume, concerning learning about racism), to more general (*Peter Pan* is really a story about Wendy and her internal struggle between wanting to stay a kid and the inevitability of growing up). And while the protagonists might begin to develop an interest in romance and figuring out their own sexuality (*Are You There God? It's Me Margaret* has scenes where the characters examine a *Playboy* and play kissing games at a party), normally it isn't the central focus. In fact, many of these books can have absolutely nothing to do with sexuality and relationships at all. There's a greater focus on growing up, on becoming able to stand on your own two feet without your parents, on learning to make good choices. MG really is about the first time you step out on your own and start making decisions for yourself, even if that decision is simply "Do we go to the corner store for candy or play road hockey?"

This is why, in most of these stories, you'll have parents who are either entirely absent or conveniently not around. The point is for the kids to have the opportunity make decisions, to have to be independent, without any help from adults.

Now, of course, this doesn't mean non-parental adults aren't present at all. Often they play the role of villain, attempting to manipulate our young hero and prevent him/her from thinking for him/herself. The villains in *Peter Pan* and *Alice in Wonderland* are Captain Hook and the Queen of Hearts respectively. In worlds of fairies and talking cats, it is a human adult who is the real danger. Adults can also be the wise sages, the ones who offer advice to a child in their moment of need, advice that the child still needs to act on for him/herself. And then there are the books where an adult comes into a child's life and helps change his/her perspective on it. Miss Honey, in *Matilda* by Roald Dahl, where Matilda finally finds someone who encourages her love of reading and makes her feel like she isn't a freak, is an excellent example.

Nonetheless, the purpose of MG is to make the kids the stars. This is their story, no one else's. And for that reason, these books can often have more whimsy and adventure in them than novels for older people. Children have a great deal of appreciation for the absurd, and they let their imaginations go wild. A good MG book can be akin to a child retelling their game of make-believe from earlier that day. Stories can be about good versus evil, magical lands, talking animals, characters that face death at every turn, and none of it needs to be qualified with cynicism, or what is known as "lampshade hanging" (TV Tropes definition: "Lampshade Hanging is the writers' trick of dealing with any element of the story that threatens the audience's willing suspension of disbelief, whether a very implausible plot development, or a particularly blatant use of a trope, by calling attention to it and simply moving on." An example of "lampshade hanging" might be something as simple as a character saying, "I know it's cliché, but I love you." The character is saying what the author fears the readers are thinking in order to be able to still say the thing the author worries might be cheesy or eye-roll worthy. In MG the author doesn't have to worry about such a cynical response to for an "I love you" for example, and can just say it without any kind of qualification.

Lastly, though MG is very much read by the kids it is aimed toward, it is similar to YA in that it can read by adults just for fun. These books, though written to be read by children, are not necessarily simplistic (though they may be simple, which is a very different thing). The language of some of these books is intrinsically beautiful, and many of them make observations in unique and clever ways. In fact, I'd argue the best MG can be read on two levels: there is usually something in a MG book that an adult can appreciate that the child reader will not notice. Take *The Phantom Tollbooth* by Norton Juster, which makes continual plays on words that children might not fully understand (at one point, the main characters find themselves in Conclusions, an island that can only be jumped to).

As far as writing MG goes, there are some restrictions that are placed on an author. While romance is allowed, there is only so far one can go with sex and romantic relationships. Profanity is usually kept to a bare minimum unless the point of the story is dealing with that language in particular, and even then it must be handled very carefully. Violence is actually far more acceptable than sexuality; there is even a place for horror, as in the Goosebumps novels of R.L. Stine. Though it is usually handled in a more practical "and then this happened" way. The more detail there is about the gore, the more it ages up the story. The actual words used in the novels don't have to be simplistic—because where better for kids to learn new words than in a book?—but more complicated words should be treated a bit like a foreign language. Add one into a sentence only now and again, and in such a way that it can be understood by the context of the sentence.

This, in a nutshell, is MG. There are exceptions to every rule, and there are also sub-categories of lower MG and upper MG. But hopefully this outline offers a basic perspective on the category.

What is YA?

YA stands for Young Adult. These novels are aimed at ages 13 and up. As with MG, YA can be aimed at different ages within that market. Further complicating things, the lines between YA and Adult can become quite blurred. This blurring, I'd argue, is due to the relative newness of the genre, and the fact that this is the first time teenagers are reading books about actual teenagers. Since teenagers have no compunctions about reading adult books, it should seem obvious that the novels that get actual teenagers interested in books about teenagers need to have qualities in common with adult novels, including writing style and theme.

More often than not, there is a great deal of confusion as to what is "allowed" and "not allowed" in a YA novel. It's an understandable question, considering the aforementioned confusion as to what YA really is, and many adults assuming it is aimed at a much younger age bracket. Fortunately, once one knows that the books are aimed at teens—those same teens who read adult novels and so on—the answer becomes quite simple: you can have whatever you want in a YA novel. Whereas MG requires certain restrictions, YA allows the writer pure freedom.

That being said, you need to understand your market. The edgier you go, the narrower an audience you are writing for. The novel *Scars* by Cheryl Rainfield, for example, is a novel that deals with sexual assault, coming to terms with one's sexual orientation and self-harm. These are all issues that many teenagers have to contend with, and the author has received fan mail from teen readers that told her this book literally saved their lives. It has also been banned in several parts of the USA because certain adults find the content objectionable. And so—like adult books, quite frankly—the less "controversial" the subject, the more likely the book will have a wider audience (which is a sad, unfortunate truth). Thus, when writing a YA book, the author must decide what kind of audience he/she is writing for, and then stick to his/her guns.

YA, like MG, is also about coming of age and firsts. But taken to an older and more mature place. Where an MG novel might be about a first kiss, a YA novel would be about losing one's virginity. In an MG novel, a protagonist might learn about racism for the first time; in YA, the main character could realize that maybe she isn't as open-minded as she initially thought. A protagonist in either MG or YA might save the world, but the YA hero might learn of the serious cost of waging war (think of the ending of *Mockingjay* by Suzanne Collins which, though positive, remains bleak). An MG ending tends be all celebrations and happily ever after. None of this, of course, is cut in stone. The *Twilight* series ends perfectly for the protagonists, and the MG series *A Series of Unfortunate Events* has an open-ended conclusion where not everything is perfectly resolved. But as a generality, the firsts experienced in YA tend to be more mature and more complex.

The one absolute must-have in a YA novel, however, is a teenaged protagonist. A YA novel is a story about a teenager, and there is simply no wiggle room there. Even if an author wishes to write about college/University, which is a very tricky subject to write about and still have one's book classified as YA—though Mariko Tamaki's *(You) Set Me On Fire* is a good example of successfully ending up in the category—the main character cannot be 20. In a world where pretty much anything goes, it's kind of nice to have one hard and fast rule. Also, as with MG, the teen protagonist must be the character who solves the problems. He/she can turn to adults, but ultimately it is the teen's story of self-discovery, no one else's.

Considering this entire book is about YA, it seems best at

this point to leave the definition alone and move on. But that's a very basic look at what YA is. And also what it isn't.

What Makes Them Similar

Now that that we have established what makes MG MG and what makes YA YA, it's important to address what makes them similar. Because it is here that we get to the crux of the confusion between the two.

The heart of the problem lies in the fact that MG and YA exist on the same continuum. They are both full-length novels, written for a market that is younger than adult, that deal with some form of coming of age. They can be set within any genre (aside from erotica). They can address a myriad of subjects. Further complicating the issue, there isn't just one particular tone that can be associated with each. That is to say, books for MG can be edgy, and YA novels can be sweet.

I would argue that out of all the factors that confuse adult readers now about the difference between the two, the coming of age factor is the big one. This is where the lines get even more blurry, and why today's adults think that we, when we were preteens, were reading what we now define as YA, when actually we weren't. People will cite Judy Blume, who wrote the ultimate period piece in *Are You There God? It's Me Margaret*. She discussed masturbation in *Deenie*. Then there was *Forever*, which was about a character losing her virginity. All these subjects are considered taboo by someone, and yet I would argue that only *Forever* could be considered an example of what we currently call YA.

Why?

It's actually an absurdly simple answer. Because despite the subject matter, or quite possibly because of it, the books were not actually aimed at 13- to 17-year-olds. *Are You There God?*

It's Me Margaret was about, amongst many things (including religion, bullying and boys), 11-year-old girls competing over who got their period first. No teen is interested in reading about something they have already had several years of experience with (or in reading about an 11-year-old). It all boils down to a simple question: would a teenager be interested in reading this? Is the main character experiencing something that the teen reader can relate to? Or how about this: When you were sixteen, what kinds of stories were you interested in reading?

Those stories were not MG. That doesn't make MG lesser, or less worthy (as an MG author myself, I am, obviously, rather fond of it), it simply means it is written for a different, equally worthy audience. In fact, it could be argued, given the evidence the incredible Ms. Judy Blume provides for us in her MG fiction, that not only can teens handle far more in their literature than some think they can, so can 8- to-12-year-olds. But that's a debate to be waged another time.

What's Next

We're still waiting to see where YA winds up positioning itself. In recent years, it's become a blockbuster of a market, launching authors into the stratosphere. Hollywood comes calling before books are even out on the shelves. But there is more going on than just big money. Many of these blockbuster books have important themes behind their popular veneer, and some of the most popular authors are dealing with some pretty big issues (witness Jay Asher writing about suicide, John Green writing about cancer). At the same time, there are also smaller books being published by smaller publishers, written by interesting and innovative authors (I refer once again to Cheryl Rainfield, whose novels are published by smaller presses, but sold thousands and were nominated for major literary awards).

The one thing we do know is that we don't know much about the future of YA. We don't know how it is going to evolve, and with New Adult now creeping up on its heels, there's still so much yet to come. So let's be like Socrates, admit we don't know anything, and stop trying to manipulate a genre that hasn't had a chance to mature yet. Young Adult is, appropriately, in its teen years. Let's see what kind of grown-up it blossoms into.

CHAPTER 2

Age Considers, Youth Ventures: Defining YA

E.C. Myers

What is YA, anyway?

Whenever the topic of young adult (YA) fiction comes up among those who are unfamiliar with it, the first question asked is usually "What makes a book YA?"

That seems like a simple enough question, but it defies a straightforward answer because there is nothing universal about the teen experience, aside from it falling within a particular age range—and even that range is sometimes debated. One tidy, albeit circular definition could be, "YA fiction features young adult characters (generally 12 to 18 years old, but sometimes 14 to 18) who are dealing with young adult concerns." Although the first half of this description satisfies the basic requirements for YA for many readers and publishers, the second half—"young adult concerns"—is no less important and demands a definition of its own, which can help distinguish YA fiction from fiction that simply features teen characters.

Concerning Young Adults

The primary requirement of a YA book is a teen protagonist, but the themes common to YA fiction are what inform whether a book belongs in this category as opposed to adult fiction or, on the other end of the spectrum, middle grade (MG) fiction.

YA books generally feature protagonists who are discovering their world and their place in it, usually as individuals. They may be confronting and questioning the things that have always known, including their relationships and their own identity, as in Scott Westerfeld's *Uglies* series, in which the metaphor of adolescent change is represented by cosmetic surgery at the age of 16 to make teens "pretty." Young Tally Youngblood at first accepts and even anticipates this fate as a natural part of life, until her friend introduces her to a different way of living and she stumbles across a government conspiracy and a group of rebels.

As part and parcel of the process of self-discovery, YA plots often involve, or are even focused on, romance. Love triangles are all too common in many YA series, with a prime example being the *Twilight* books by Stephenie Meyer, which divided readers into "Team Edward" and "Team Jacob" according to who they though the protagonist, Bella Swan, should end up with.

Adult characters, especially parents, are sidelined or missing, giving the YA protagonists the freedom to be on their own — while other adult authority figures are distrusted or serve as antagonists. The Chaos Walking books by Patrick Ness, beginning with *The Knife of Never Letting Go*, pits 13-year-old Todd Hewitt, the last boy in Prentisstown, directly against its mayor and the other adult men, forced to survive on his own after his adoptive parents try to send him away to safety.

Core to the conflict in a good YA book are clear personal stakes and protagonists who play an active role in changing their lives and/or societies. In keeping with the "Chosen One" trope in popular culture, the main character may be special or different in some way, becoming a key agent of that change, as in the *His Dark Materials* books by Philip Pullman. In the first book of the trilogy, *The Golden Compass*, Lyra Belacqua, 12 years old, learns that she has been prophesied to "bring about the end of destiny," and finds that she is the only person who knows how to use a mystical device called the alethiometer. As in stories of this type, she easily rallies others to support her, united by a common cause.

While most fiction protagonists regardless of their age will have the most to lose and the most to gain, YA characters will feel more, and more intensely, than a protagonist in an adult book might. Their feelings are inextricably caught up in their situation and often inform the outcome, making this very much a personal, emotional journey. The conclusion of Gayle Forman's *If I Stay* hinges on 17-year-old Mia's decision on whether to return to her body and face a difficult life after a tragic car accident kills her family and propels her into an out of body experience.

How then, does YA differ from coming of age stories written for adults? Although most YA certainly can be described as a coming of age—the psychological transition from childhood to adulthood—not all coming-of-age stories are YA. In adult literature, a coming of age tale is referred to as a bildungsroman, largely focused on character growth, developing maturity, and ultimately acceptance of a place in society. The goal of the entire story may be this personal and emotional change, while YA may have more of an emphasis on achieving some external change as well.

Young protagonists in adult fiction commonly are more passive than in YA, observers of their own stories—quite literally in the case of *The Lovely Bones* by Alice Sebold, in which 14-year-old Susie Salmon watches from Heaven after she is raped and murdered. These books have the retrospective quality of memoir, either implied in the voice or more explicitly written from an adult perspective looking back on young adulthood and the moment that everything changed.

The key distinction, then, is in the point of view and the immediacy of the events as they unfold, and whether the tone is instructive or educational (in a bildungsroman, the protagonist may be relating a learned lesson or reflecting on earned maturity) or emotional (as in YA, where the protagonist is experiencing events in the moment, at the same time as the reader). The goals of the protagonists, then, align with the goals of the author in writing the book, whether she intends to relate an experience or revelations that are more relevant to other adults or meaningful to teen readers.

Consider Your Audience

Complicating the concept of authorial intent in defining YA is the fact that sometimes books sold or marketed as YA were originally intended for adult readers, not written specifically to speak to teen readers. For example, *Cures for Heartbreak* by Margo Rabb was written as a literary novel for adults but was sold and marketed as YA. In it, 15-year-old Mia Perlman is struggling to cope with the sudden death of her mother from cancer and her father's hospitalization following a heart attack. With the life she knew gone, Mia seeks comfort and a new identity for herself, and forges new relationships with her family and some new friends. The grief she feels resonates with young adults and adults alike, whether or not they have experienced such deep losses of their own, but the raw emotion and the fact that the narrative is grounded firmly in the moment as we follow Mia's journey of discovery is what places it clearly on the young side of the YA divide.

This "rebranding" or positioning of adult books to appeal to YA audiences can also take place long after the book has been published for the first time. The quintessential example of this is J.D. Salinger's *The Catcher in the Rye*, which has a teenage protagonist and is assigned reading in high schools across the U.S. Though this book was written for adults—in 1951, well before the YA category was formalized—it is often cited as the predecessor for today's concept of YA. David Levithan, YA author and editor at Scholastic, tells us why: "Holden Caulfield is the embodiment of what we mean by the phrase 'young adult'—too young to be a grown-up, but too wise to the world to be completely innocent. He's caught in the in-between, and that in-between is what all young adult authors write about." Naturally, others disagree with designating *The Catcher in the Rye* as YA; author Bruce Brooks proposes that it is a lack of change in Holden Caulfield that disqualifies it from this category, despite its otherwise authentic young adult voice and appeal.

Another example of rebranding for younger readers is *Ender's Game* by Orson Scott Card, which these days may be found in both the adult science fiction shelves as well as children's sections, with nothing changed but the cover. Although the mature themes and school setting help connect the book to teen readers, Ender Wiggin and his classmates enter Battle School to train to fight aliens at only 6 years old; although this breaks the one rule of YA—that it feature teen protagonists—these 6-year-olds are precocious enough that they act at least twice their age. But obviously this book was never intended for readers of that age or even MG audiences, let alone teens.

It seems that if a book can be marketed as YA then chances are it will be, likely because right now, YA sells, and marketing a book as such may improve your chances of getting it published. The overwhelming popularity of J.K. Rowling's Harry Potter series gave adults "permission" to read children's fiction and has largely been held responsible for the YA fiction boom in the last couple of decades (Smith, 2012). In fact, studies show that adults reportedly now make up more than 50 percent of YA buyers (Keener, 2013). Certainly from a financial standpoint, publishers are keenly interested in discovering the "next Harry Potter," to capitalize on the growing base of YA readers (Sporkin, 2013). But even with the added incentive of imagined riches for YA authors, just because a book has YA-age characters does not mean it can or should be marketed as a young adult book.

Young vs. Adult

To illustrate the importance of theme in determining whether a book with a YA-age point of view character is meant for children or adults, consider the novel *Ready Player One* by Ernest Cline. Wade Owen Watts, age 18, is forced to live on his own after his family is tragically killed. Like many in his world, he is obsessed with an online simulation game called OASIS. As his virtual persona, Parzival, he works to solve a puzzle challenge left by the deceased creator of OASIS that only the most knowledgeable and skilled player can hope to win—and Parzival soon proves himself up to the task.

At its most basic, this is an ideal setup for a YA novel; however, Wade is unlike most YA protagonists in that he is not truly coming of age or wondering where he fits into his world. When the novel opens, he is already well versed in the rules of the dystopian society he lives in and subverting them as he can. His character does evolve through the course of the book, as he learns to trust and work with his opponents in the game, but the focus remains squarely on his efforts to win.

Mentally, Wade is basically already an adult, albeit a maladjusted one that needs to work on his social skills outside of the game. Romance is also a feature, but not a major plot point, and the novel is steeped heavily in nostalgia that means more to geeks who grew up in the 1970s and 1980s than with contemporary teens. Overall, the book is more about revealing the world and how it works to readers rather than Wade. It revels in the possibilities of the game and has fun with the premise, with less emphasis on following Wade on some emotional journey.

Contrast this with *The Hunger Games* by Suzanne Collins, which presents another dystopian future society preoccupied with a different game. Sixteen-year-old Katniss Everdeen *thinks* that she knows the ways of her world, having adapted to the rough life in remote District 12. But when she volunteers in her younger sister's place to participate in the annual Hunger Games, which pits twenty-four representatives from all 12 districts against each other until there is only one survivor, she discovers just how corrupt and decadent her country's leaders are.

Katniss learns about the Capitol for the first time and how the games work on the inside; like Wade in *Ready Player One*, she also must trust her opponents and forge new friendships, but the stakes are higher: All of their lives are on the line. She also faces the realization that her own government is the enemy and those sponsoring the games are the enemy, and everything they have been taught has been a lie.

A romantic plotline is central to *The Hunger Games*, evoking another trope of YA fiction, the love triangle. Though Katniss' character arc develops over the course of the trilogy, an important aspect of this first book is her acceptance of her role in the Games and society and her efforts to protect herself and the people she loves: her family (especially her sister); her main love interest, Peeta; and her best friend, Gale.

Ready Player One and *The Hunger Games* are both nominally adventure stories about the main characters trying to win a game, but they are fundamentally different, most tellingly in terms of their attention to emotion. Katniss is much more introspective and preoccupied by her feelings, while Wade is primarily driven by his obsession and ambition. This is not a difference in what defines a "boy book" or a "girl book," despite the genders of their respective POV characters, but a more striking comparison between books meant for teen readers and those meant for adults. There is a greater immediacy to many YA novels and a sense that they are risking more, with significant personal consequences for their actions.

Another interesting distinction is in their differing approaches to world building. Both books feature science fictional worlds different from our own, but *The Hunger Games* describes it to readers in a much more natural way, through Katniss' eyes, while in *Ready Player One*, Wade directly addresses the readers and describes his world in sometimes too-loving detail. A focus on character over world building and limited exposition is indicative of most good YA novels, perhaps because teen readers are less patient than many adult readers and demand a faster pace and more streamlined storytelling, as pointed out by author Diana Wynne Jones:

Children are used to making an effort to understand. They are asked for this effort every hour of every school day and, though they may not make the effort willingly, they at least expect it. In addition, nearly everyone between the ages of nine and fifteen is amazingly good at solving puzzles and following complicated plots—this being the happy result of many hours spent at computer games and watching television (Jones, 1990).

Ready Player One also relies on a shared pop culture history with its intended readers, which includes *Dungeons and Dragons*, the movie *War Games,* and TV shows like *Family Ties* — dated frames of reference that most teen readers would be unfamiliar with. Meanwhile, *The Hunger Games* perhaps best capitalizes on younger readers' relative inexperience with a well-worn history of dystopian fiction and survival games. A reader who had read the Japanese novel *Battle Royale* or seen its movie adaptation would come to *The Hunger Games* with a different set of expectations than one who hadn't. Identifying the assumed common knowledge base helps determine the intended audience of a book.

Nonetheless, because of the younger age of the majority of the characters in *Ready Player One*, who could be considered special in their world and are also struggling against a corporation that will threaten their way of life, this book has been considered a "crossover" book that may appeal to teen readers. Books with YA characters and certain types of content, such as adventure stories or fantasy novels featuring magic, are often marketed to YA readers, though they are published as adult books. The annual Alex Awards, presented by Young Adult Library Services Association, identify and celebrate the best books written for adults that teens will also enjoy, titles such as *The Magicians* by Lev Grossman (which features a college-age protagonist), *Mr. Penumbra's 24-Hour Bookstore* by Robin Sloan (an adult protagonist), and *The Night Circus* by Erin Morgenstern (protagonists of all ages with an omniscient narrator).

Some adult books with young adult characters may meet both the age and theme requirements, yet still not be considered YA; for example, *The End of Everything* by Megan Abbott (Jensen). The protagonist is 13-year-old Lizzie Hood, whose life gets turned upside down when her best friend, Evie, mysteriously disappears—seemingly abducted. As she investigates her missing friend's life, she discovers that Evie wasn't the person or the friend she'd always thought she was. The point of view is tight on Lizzie, who tells the story in first person, but it is narrated from an adult Lizzie, many years following the events in the book. This distanced perspective positions the novel firmly as a coming-of-age story for adults, which looks back on and interprets the events through the lens of adult experience. This book is firmly intended for adult readers. Memoir stories like *The End of Everything*, however well they might capture a teen experience or voice, are at a remove from young adult readers because the full consequences of the protagonist's actions and the outcomes of events are already known, instead of looking at them through the character's eyes in the moment, from a point of uncertainty. Moreover, the story takes place in the late 1980s, which makes it much more likely to resonate with adult readers today than contemporary teenagers, much like *Ready Player One*.

A big component of the YA versus adult discussion concerns something known as the "YA voice." This may mean that the narrator sounds like a plausible teenager, or that the dialogue reminds you of the teenager you were or teens you've met. But this broad statement is essentially the equivalent of "you know it when you see it." YA is YA because the elements of the story work together to create a certain feeling in the reader that connects somehow with the teen experience; if enough of those elements are in place, the story will "feel" YA. Some common characteristics of the majority of YA fiction include a shorter length (the sweet spot is about 80,000 words); more straightforward, approachable prose; faster pacing; protagonists with more agency; protagonists experiencing "firsts" like their first time on their own, their first love, their first time having sex, their first breakup, and so on. But these aren't rules, they're ingredients which can flavor the basic recipe. As always, making any generalizations about YA come with the usual disclaimers: there are always exceptions, your mileage may vary.

How Adult is Too Adult for YA?

Often, what people mean when they ask "What is YA?" is "What is appropriate content for a YA book?" Typically, they're concerned about whether it's okay to include sex, bad language, violence — things that some parents and schools think kids shouldn't be exposed to in works of fiction, whether or not they are prevalent in society or address issues concerning today's teens. A recurring criticism in recent years has been that YA has become too dark, featuring more sex, violence, and death than children's books used to contain, in an effort to "keep books relevant for the young" (Gurdon, 2011).

Popular, critically acclaimed, and award-winning YA books like *The Absolutely True Diary of a Part-Time Indian* by Sherman Alexie, *Looking for Alaska* by John Green, and *The Perks of Being a Wallflower* by Stephen Chbosky are routinely challenged or banned from schools and libraries for inappropriate content (ALA); however, in general, varying degrees of sex, language, and violence—or any other topic or content that you might expect to find in books for adults—are by no means off-limits to YA fiction. For example, *Boy Toy* by Barry Lyga was considered somewhat controversial for including some uncomfortably graphic sex scenes between a teacher and an underage student, but the sex was not gratuitous, and in fact the title won the 2007 Cybil Award and made the YALSA Best Books for Young Adults list in 2008.

In short, any language or behavior that makes sense for the characters and is essential to the story is permissible, although YA does trend toward being less graphic, at least in sexual content. Again, this is primarily a marketing concern, and a graphic or potentially controversial scene that serves an important purpose in the story wouldn't balk most publishers.

YA is a Label

Because every novel is unique and many do not clearly fit into one category or another, the most reliable way to tell if a particular book is intended for young adult readers is to look at its cover or copyright page or the publisher's website. YA imprints are usually easy to identify, featuring words like "children," "kids," "teen," "young readers" and so on (McNally 2013). Thus, the only true criterion for YA is the publisher's (and not necessarily the author's) target audience for the book, making YA essentially nothing more than a marketing category.

In some ways, it may seem easier to define YA by what it is *not*, systematically refuting the efforts of some to impose clear restrictions on their themes and content and assume a lesser quality or worth. Here is another sticking point: *YA is not a genre*. It is a marketing category, within which you can find the same range of genres that fill adult shelves, including but never limited to contemporary, science fiction, fantasy, horror, paranormal romance, historical, and so much more. Until a few years ago, all YA books were generally shelved together in libraries and bookstores, regardless of their genre; only recently have Barnes & Noble stores begun subcategorizing books according to "Teen Fantasy and Adventure" and "Teen Paranormal" and "Stories of Survival," in an effort to point readers to more books similar to the ones they know they like. Often, a YA author will write across genres without concern about losing readers, because teens will read anything and everything.

The defining characteristics of YA and adult fiction are being subverted further with the newest marketing category to be announced: "New Adult." Often described as "YA with sex," the distinction is actually just as nuanced as distinguishing YA from other categories; New Adult books feature older, college-age protagonists (age 18 to 25), dealing with different questions of identity and a certain level of cynicism that is lacking from the more hopeful, idealistic YA fiction (Kaufman, 2012). And yes, there's more sex.

A better question than "What is YA?" might be "Why must we define YA?" If YA is purely a matter of marketing, merely an artificial and fluid construct designed to help sell books to certain audiences, then authors should just write whatever they want—telling the stories the way they need to be told—and worry about categorizing them later, leaving it to agents, editors, and publishers to figure out how to sell it. Besides, it's a rule of thumb that kids will "read up," so that children younger than 14 may be reading YA books intended for more mature readers—which means many teens may not be reading YA at all! Essentially, teens will read whatever they want, including middle grade and adult books, and surely even new adult; only adults seem concerned about fitting YA into its own neat category.

Perhaps a better, easier, and more straightforward answer to the question, "What is YA?" is this: YA is what you should be reading.

Any writer who wants to build a career in writing YA fiction must be familiar with the category, in all its varied genres. Read widely to get a sense of trends. Not necessarily trends in the type of books being published, such as vampires or dystopian, though this also can be helpful if you are concerned about how marketable your work might be, but to get a solid impression of the way teens are portrayed, mastering the correct voice, learning the right balance of world building and exposition, how relationships are presented, and so on—so that you'll know it when you see it, and write it. Ideally, anyone writing YA also reads YA, and preferably *loves* reading YA.

Of course, writers should read everything, but it is especially important to read the very best YA being published today to avoid making the wrong assumptions about it. YA books are not easier to write than books for adults. YA books should not be "dumbed down" for younger readers. YA books do not need to eschew sex, violence, and language. Treat your readers with respect, and above all, *write well.*

CHAPTER 3

The Problem With Parents

Deby Fredericks

Part I: Once Upon A Time...

...I was at a barbecue with some friends. The conversation came around to children's books, and my friend Brad asked, "How come, in these stories, the parents are always gone? Shouldn't they be keeping track of what their kids are doing?"

And I said, "What fun would that be?"

We all laughed, but the question is an excellent one. Why are the parents in YA books so often missing in action? They're either dead, absent for some reason, or so flighty that they might as well not be there.

Well, there are two reasons, as closely related as parent and child.

REASON #1: THIS IS A CHILDREN'S BOOK! The kid is the

star of the show. Whether the kid is five or fifteen, he should be the one who notices the problem, investigates it, and takes action.

Running against this is a little thing called biology.

Have you ever seen a bunch of ducklings following their mother around? That's how they learn what it takes to be a duck. Well, people do this, too. The old saw, "Monkey see, monkey do?" It's perfectly true, and it's a problem for writers because…

REASON #2: PARENTS ARE BOSSY! They always take over. I don't mean that in a sinister way. Parents love their kids. If something is going on, the parents want to protect their family.

So kids are programmed to go to their parents when they have problems. Once they do that, the parents tell them exactly what to do, and usually the kids will do it. Soon all is well.

This is completely realistic and normal—and it makes for a very boring story. Worse, these adults, with the best of intentions, will do *everything* for the kids.

Say the child protagonist suspects their cat has been replaced by an alien doppelganger. (Hey, it could happen! In fact, many people already suspect that cats are secretly our alien overlords.) The child runs to the parents, crying, "Fluffy has a ray-gun, and she's coming this way!"

The parents spring into action. They shove the child into the nearest bedroom, lock it, then run out to confront the feline invader. Very noble.

Well, if the child is supposed to be the star, how can they shine when they're locked in the bedroom? For a children's book to be satisfying (or any book, really), the protagonist has to be the one calling the shots. Everyone else has to get out of the way.

And this, Brad, is why the parents are never there.

BY THE WAY…When I speak of parents, I really mean any adults in your story. Teachers, police officers, grandparents, aunts and uncles, counselors, preachers, even well-meaning strangers. All have the potential to dominate kids.

Part II: Coping Strategies

There's really no escaping the "parent problem." Our characters may spring from our imaginations, but they don't exist in a vacuum. Any fictional background is going to include parents and family. What's a poor writer to do?

Here are a few time-honored strategies for keeping the parents from hogging the spotlight.

DEAD AND GONE (A). Kind of says it all. The parents have either died or they are somewhere far away. This can apply to a workaholic parent or a parent who's in jail, but most often one or both parents have actually died prior to the beginning of the story.

Examples: In the saga of Spider-Man, Peter Parker's parents are dead. He's being raised by his aunt and uncle. Batman's parents were shot before his eyes when he was eight years old. In fact, Superman's whole *planet* blew up when he was six months old.

(Are we seeing a theme here? Don't let your kids grow up to be super-heroes. You'll die!!)

DISTRACTED (B). These are parents who don't pay any attention to what their kids are doing. They're on the phone, they're busy matching socks, whatever. Even when the kid runs up to tell them Fluffy has a ray-gun, they just chuckle and pat him on the head.

Sometimes the kid really is that much smarter than his parents, but usually it's just that the parents are as smart as a bag of rocks.

Example: In *The Hunger Games*, Katniss's father has died and her mother fallen into abject depression. This leaves Katniss to take care of her little sister and her mother at the same time.

DISAPPROVING (C). The parents disapprove of something about their child. Maybe they want the kid to take part in a sport he hates, or the kid's grades might not be up to par, or they're afraid of his super-power. Their disapproval has created enough of a rift that the kid is not willing to share what's going on.

Examples: In Anne McCaffrey's *Dragonsong*, Menolly adores music, but her parents discourage her because they don't believe a girl can have a career as a Harper.

Throughout the *Harry Potter* series, the title character battles his aunt and uncle's prejudice against wizards.

ROAD TRIP (D). In this case it's the kids who leave, while the parents stay behind. Whether they run away or find themselves transported to a magical world, the adults are not able to intrude into the events of the story.

Examples: In *The Lion, the Witch, and the Wardrobe*, by C.S. Lewis, London is being bombed, so the four Pevensey kids are sent to live in the country. Thanks to a magical armoire, they travel a bit farther than expected.

In *The Frog Princess*, by E.D. Baker, the title character is turned into a frog and stranded in the middle of a swamp.

TWISTED (E). This is a step beyond disapproval, to parents who are really mean or openly malicious toward the child. It can also encompass dystopian systems where the entire government is malevolent. If a kid asked these parents for advice, they wouldn't get it—or the advice would make the situation even more dangerous.

Examples: In *A Series of Unfortunate Events*, three orphans fall into the clutches of the wicked Count Olaf, who schemes to take their inheritance for himself.

In *Captain Underpants*, two bright young boys are surrounded by a school full of the most awful teachers and staff imaginable.

RIVALRY (F). Similar to Distracted, but there is someone or something who actively competes with the child protagonist for the parents' attention. Perhaps a sibling is seriously ill, or Grandma is so obsessed with World Wrestling that she doesn't notice the ray-gun-wielding alien cats.

Examples: In the *Harry Potter* series, Harry's cousin Dudley is spoiled and demanding. If Harry gets anything worth having, Dudley moves immediately to take it away.

Part III: Mix And Match

There are all kinds of ways to combine these strategies. For instance, in *Dragonsong*, Menolly's disapproving parents (C) finally drive her to run away (D), and that's when her real adventures begin. In *A Series of Unfortunate Events*, the Beaudelaire kids are orphaned (A), and this leads to their struggles with Olaf (E). Having more than one challenge can be good for your book. It keeps trouble coming at your characters on more than one front.

Some of you have probably already realized that the Harry Potter series utilizes almost every one of these strategies. (A) Harry's parents are dead, (B) Professor McGonagall routinely discounts Harry's warnings, (C) Uncle Vernon despises all wizards, (D) Harry is invited/escapes to Hogwarts, (E) Professor Snape does everything he can to hold Harry back, and (F) Dudley is Harry's rival.

There's a problem here. Can you spot it?

(I'll hum the Jeopardy song while you work it out...)

Here's a hint: Too much of a good thing can become a bad

thing. (Humming the second refrain...)

Okay, got it?

The problem is that there are so many plot devices at work. It all piles up. If you're even a little bit cynical, it becomes ridiculous. Rowling managed to balance it all because she had seven long books to work with. For those of us just trying to finish our first novels, it's better to choose one tactic and follow it through.

Less is more, little Grasshopper.

Another problem with such pat strategies is the potential to irritate your audience. Although kids and teens are still the target readers, more and more grown-ups read YA books. The subject matter is gripping, the story-telling is great, and they're short, so time-pressed adults can squeeze them into our schedules.

Speaking as an adult reader of YA, I can tell you the grown-ups will pick up on certain things. Like when the mean parents cross the line to actual neglect or abuse. Or when all the adult characters are conveniently stupid to make the kids look smarter.

Please don't do that. We can tell when we're being insulted, thanks.

Part IV: Bridging Troubled Waters

Although these plot devices serve the purpose of getting the adults out of the way so the child protagonist can shine, they all share a nagging weakness: It's too evident that they are devices.

I've already mentioned that the inborn impulse is for adults to lead and kids to follow. Because of this, the reader recognizes that something is amiss when they read about George and Harold's principal stalking them, looking for an excuse to give them detention.

As a writer, you may have laid out your entire situation and justified all the reactions, but it doesn't matter if the reader stops paying attention to your story because they're so busy thinking, "That's not right."

And yet, you still need to keep the parents from taking over the book. Is there no hope??

Yes, Virginia, There's Always Hope!

I can suggest two alternative approaches. I know, you're all creative writers. You'll probably think of your own approaches. (Try them first. One's own ideas are always the best.) These are mine, just as something to think about.

1. Don't treat the adults as quick stereotypes. All the characters should be treated equally. Give them a chance to speak their point of view. Even if the child protagonist isn't going to follow the parent's advice, a reasoned argument ramps up the pressure.

Think about it. It's easy to defy a mean adult who is screeching at you. It's much harder to disobey good advice given by a loving mother or father. Your child reader knows this. Most of them have experienced this exact conflict, so your child protagonist's situation will resonate with them.

It takes a really brave child to act against their parent's wishes. Your readers will love seeing a fellow kid do what she believes is right, even if it means breaking the rules.

2. Offer alternative parenting. Human beings are social creatures. A child without parents has to fill a big hole in his life. This is why, in the real world, so many young men without fathers join gangs.

Use this in your story. You don't have to explain all about it; readers will understand the drive to find an emotional home.

For instance, in *Superman*, the title character's parents couldn't escape the destruction of Krypton. He arrives on

Earth alone, but luckily is found by the Kents, a childless couple who raise him as their own.

In the fantasy animé, *Record of Lodoss War*, Parn's father is a knight who goes to war and never returns. Through the series, Parn searches for a father-figure. He finds one first in the Dwarf warrior Ghim, and later in dashing King Kashu.

3. Don't treat the separation as a quick and easy way to get on with your story. Really think about the family dynamic. Make it a strong part of your plot.

Part V: Setting An Example

To illustrate what I mean, let's look at two examples: a contemporary fantasy series, and the classic novel *Charlotte's Web*.

FIRST EXAMPLE: *Tales of the Frog Princess*, a humorous poke at fairy tales written by E. D. Baker.

Book 1, *The Frog Princess*, starts with Princess Emma at odds with her mother. Queen Chartreuse orders her to marry Prince Jorge, a man she doesn't like. Emma turns for comfort to her Aunt Grassina, the Green Witch. Shortly afterward, Emma kisses an enchanted frog. Instead of restoring Eadric's humanity, Emma also gets turned into a frog! With the help of some animal friends, Emma and Eadric make their way back to Grassina, who helps them both return to normal.

In Book 2, *Dragon's Breath*, Emma's mother refuses her wish to break her engagement with Jorge so she can marry Eadric. Grassina asks for Emma's help to restore her fiancee, Haywood, who was turned into an otter by Grassina's wicked-witch mother, Olivene. After many trials, they succeed, but Olivene makes sure Grassina is struck by the family's curse.

Kind and beautiful Grassina instantly turns ugly and wicked; the mantle of Green Witch passes to Emma, who must defend her kingdom against Prince Jorge's army.

On to Book 3, *Once Upon a Curse*, where Chartreuse, still disapproving, wants Emma to hurry up and marry Eadric. Meanwhile, Grassina's wicked magic is becoming a problem. Emma and Eadric travel in time to prevent the curse being cast on Emma and Grassina's ancestor. In doing so, they restore both Olivene and Grassina to the good women they once were. Since Chartreuse no longer feels the dread of the curse, she is able to accept Emma for who she is.

Not only is there a plot arc within each book, all three together have a plot art covering Emma's transition from a typical spirited princess with a disapproving mother to a powerful sorceress who is fit to rule her kingdom one day.

SECOND EXAMPLE: The ultimate classic children's book, *Charlotte's Web*, shows how the author hit almost every note perfectly.

1. Fern's parents show respect. Not deference! Respect.

In the very first line, Fern asks why Pa has an axe. Ma doesn't ignore her question or try to sugar-coat the situation with the baby pig. She respects Fern's ability to understand difficult problems.

2. White lets all the characters speak for themselves.

In *Charlotte's Web*, the parents give their point of view, and they listen to Fern's viewpoint. Pa listens to Fern's plea but explains that he doesn't have time to take care of a sickly piglet.

3. Ma and Pa don't try to solve Fern's problems for her.

Fern is still upset and wants to save the piglet. Again, Pa doesn't brush her feelings aside. Instead, he challenges Fern to take care of the piglet herself.

For her part, Ma gives Fern what she needs to take care of Wilbur, but she doesn't offer any help beyond that. The actual tasks are up to Fern.

4. Parents support the child and recognize her success.

Although they don't lavishly praise Fern, it's clear from the context that they approve of the outcome. Although Charlotte does a lot of the work, it's Fern who learns the most from helping Wilbur. For one thing, she ends up working with things like rats and spiders, which she might otherwise run away from.

Part VI: Yeah, But...

Some of you, as you listen to me pontificating about plot arcs and role models, may have found yourselves thinking, "Yeah, but…"

" …*Charlotte's Web*? That's so 20th Century! My book isn't all wholesome like that. I'm writing edgy, gritty, dark!"

So write it edgy, gritty and dark. It's your story. Nobody else can tell you how to write it.

" …What do you mean, the adults can't be conveniently stupid? It's every child's dream to be smarter than the grown-ups!"

Um, sure. See above. Just don't whine to me when you get reviews that comment on how conveniently stupid the grown-ups are acting.

" …Sometimes adults really are mean for no reason."

To the child, happily playing video games, it might seem kind of random for their parents to walk in and ask about their homework or tell them to come have dinner.

Well, it's not random. Somehow you have to imply that, or your plot will feel flimsy.

I can't stress this enough. In a successful story, nothing happens at random. Every image, every event, every line of dialogue should focus to make the point you want.

Part VII: One Last Thing

If I could impart just one wise thought to aspiring Young Adult writers, it would be this: the relationship between parents and kids is rich and deep and powerful. *Use it for all you can get.*

CHAPTER 4

Writing YA Science Fiction as if Science Matters

Allen Steele

Some years ago, I was invited to a meeting of school librarians from western Massachusetts, where I'd recently become a resident. They wanted advice from a professional science fiction author about a problem they were facing: the shortage of good young-adult SF.

We met at the regional library in Hatfield, only a stone's throw from the home of my friend and colleague Jane Yolen. About a dozen librarians showed up, and while only a few were familiar with my work, it soon became apparent that most had at least some knowledge of science fiction, and several were regular readers. So it wasn't as if I had to tell them who Isaac Asimov was or that *Dune* is one of the greatest SF novels ever written; they knew that already. Nonetheless, they were stumped. The Harry Potter series had lured a lot of kids into reading for pleasure—for this, at least, we owe J.K. Rowling a vast debt—but while there were mountains of fantasy novels meant for teenagers, there seemed to be precious little SF for the same audience. Most of the kids had already found classics like *A Wrinkle in Time*, and the librarians were reluctant to give them *Star Wars* tie-ins and the like, but what else was out there? That's what they wanted me to tell them.

I dug deep into my memory for the books I'd read and enjoyed when I was a kid, and soon discovered something that surprised me: nearly every title I recommended was either out of print and hence unavailable, or so dated that it would have been like giving *Tom Swift and His Motor Boat* to a boy who'd spent last summer hotdogging about a lake on his uncle's JetSki. I knew from a recent speaking gig at MIT with Orson Scott Card that quite a few students there were fans of *Ender's Game*, but many of the librarians were reluctant to put it on their shelves; its violence and sex was the sort of content liable to draw the wrath of sensitive parents.

As a result, the list we compiled began with Robert A. Heinlein and ended with Andre Norton, with very little else in-between. That's when I realized that there was a paucity of contemporary young-adult SF, and someone should be writing this stuff.

It took a while to get around to doing just that—I'd just begun work on *Coyote*, my best-known novel, and its success led me to spend most of the next decade turning it into a series—and by the time I wrote my first YA novel, *Apollo's Outcasts*, the situation had changed. While fantasy still vastly outnumbers science fiction in the YA section of most bookstores and libraries, SF has recently experienced a resurgence. *The Hunger Games* trilogy has become nearly as popular as the Harry Potter books—when I saw the movie adaptation of the first book, it was in a theater filled with teenagers who'd already read both it and its sequels—and novels like Cory Doctorow's *Little Brother* and Paolo Bacigalupi's *Ship Breaker* have become bestsellers. So while those librarians I met may still have to wade through stacks of books about medieval princesses and their pet dragons, neither do they have to settle for novels written decades ago by Heinlein and Norton.

However, there's a couple of problems with much of the young-adult SF being published today. The first is overused settings and thematic clichés; the second is lack of scientific or technological credibility.

In a way, both are actually aspects of a single problem, one which poses a challenge to anyone setting out to write science fiction for a teenage audience. Meeting that challenge is what this essay is about.

It's hardly a revelation that dystopias are the prevalent themes of much current YA science fiction. Success breeds imitation, so we can blame editors who are more interested in duplication than innovation for dozens of novels set in gritty, torn-up societies run by tyrants or evil corporations, which have become as commonplace as sexy teenage vampires.

Running second but catching up are novels set on Mars. About half are self-published Kindle ebooks, yet mainstream publishers have discovered this trend as well. I was contemplating a Mars novel of my own until I discovered that the red planet has lately become oft-visited territory, and another book about a teenager who goes to Mars would be as redundant as another book about a kid who discovers that he's a vampire, werewolf, zombie, etc.

This is not to say that all dystopian or Martian YA novels are repetitious or derivative. Many are worthwhile; I recommend *Ship Breaker* or John Barnes' *Losers in Space* without reservation.

But both Bacigalupi and Barnes are established SF authors familiar with the creative discipline necessary to write good, original science fiction. Which leads us to the second problem: lack of scientific or technological credibility.

It's easy to see why *The Hunger Games* trilogy has become a roaring success. The novels are compellingly readable, fast-moving and well-plotted, with memorable characters and striking settings. I enjoyed each one. As science fiction, though, they leave much to be desired. Particularly in the first book, Collins often displays a embarrassing lack of awareness of some basic technological concepts. For example, she often calls vertical take-off and landing aircraft (VTOLs) "hovercraft," which are a different thing entirely; hovercraft don't fly, but instead are ground-effect vehicles which float a few inches off the surface via high-speed rotors or magnetic levitation. Cloning is a long and difficult process; you can't take a dead body, remove some cells from it, and within a few hours transform them into a chimera (i.e, a bioengineered amalgam of human and animal). And then there's stuff that's more supernatural than scientific. Food and drink instantly materialize upon spoken command; artificially-incurred floods and forest fires occur spontaneously, then stop just as suddenly without residual after-effects.

Underlying these and other gaffs is a misunderstanding of Clarke's Third Law. As expressed by Sir Arthur C. Clarke, it states: "Any sufficiently advanced technology is indistinguishable from magic." This is a major principle behind much modern science fiction, but also one often interpreted the wrong way by those who evoke it. The key concept here is appearance; although something might *seem* to be magical, nonetheless there has to be some technological or scientific rationale behind it. You can't simply have something magical occur, then claim that it's really a form of advanced technology; there must be a reason why it happens that doesn't depend on supernatural forces.

This is the major difference between science fiction and fantasy. Take a flying carpet, for instance. If you stand beside a carpet, recite an arcane incantation you learned at Hogwarts and get it to rise from the floor, then that's fantasy. But if you attach wings and an engine to it, provide it with fuel and a control system, you might be able to make it fly—probably not very well, but it'll fly nonetheless. That's science fiction.

There's nothing wrong with fantasy, so long as the reader understands that it's such. But to write a fantasy story and then claim that it's science fiction because it appears to follow Clarke's Third Law only shows that you don't really understand what Clarke meant. Technobabble—the use of scientific-sounding terminology that doesn't really mean anything—is just a not-so-clever form of disguise. If you can't explain the terminology you're using, then it's mere camouflage.

To effectively write science fiction of any sort means doing research—the more, the better. And to write science fiction for a teenage readership means that you have to be particularly careful how you do your research and the way you present what you've learned. Kids are curious. When they read something that sparks their interest, they're likely to investigate further. In this day and age, they're only a few keystrokes away from looking something up with a Google search. If they discover that you got something wrong, they're not liable to be as forgiving as an adult reader might be.

The trick is to do your homework so well that your story's factual background is bulletproof...and then use only what you need to tell your story. One thing that can bog down a novel to the point where a reader gets bored and puts it down is an overabundance of scientific detail, yet it's tempting for a writer who's spent months on research to include everything he or she learned.

This isn't easy. Even the best writers can let their research get the better of them. Robert A. Heinlein's classic "juveniles" are often considered the gold standard for YA science fiction, and for good reason; he was an absolute master of writing for young people without talking down to them (the cardinal rule of writing YA fiction of any kind). But in *Have Spacesuit, Will Travel*—arguably his best YA novel—there's a chapter where Heinlein spent ten pages having his protagonist, Kip, describe in intricate detail the process by which he restored the second-hand spacesuit he won in a contest. It's all drop-dead accurate, right down to the breathing mixture, but my eyes glazed over when I read this as a kid, and I had much the same reaction when I re-read the novel as an adult. The rest of the novel is terrific…but I wonder how many teenagers today would put the book down in the middle of Chapter Three and not pick it up again.

If you do it right, though, then you get a story that has a such sense of verisimilitude that even the unlikely seems real. If you can achieve that, you can hook and draw in even the reader who thought he or she wouldn't like a science fiction novel.

Over the years, I've developed a three-step process for writing science fiction:

First, do your research, and do it carefully. If the subject matter is complex, then read everything about it you can lay your hands on: college texts, popular science books, magazine and newspaper articles, dedicated web sites. Often I'll compile a list of the things I need to investigate, and then work my way through the list, using Google and Amazon to track down primary sources. If necessary, I'll email experts and ask for their advice. On occasion, I may even travel to places— because I often write about space exploration, I've been to NASA facilities like Cape Canaveral or the Marshall Space Flight Center more times than I can remember—and take notes. Less complex material, or incidental facts, doesn't need as much investigation, but I'll look anyway…and everything gets checked twice, all the way through the rewrites and final editing process. I may make a mistake now and then—everyone does—but it isn't for lack of trying.

(Incidentally, the worst way to research a science fiction novel is by reading science fiction novels. All you're going to do is repeat the same errors other writers before you have made. For instance, it wasn't until I began researching Dyson spheres by tracking down and reading Freeman Dyson's original 1960 letter-essay to *Science* that I discovered that every nearly SF writer since then has gotten his concept wrong. Reading other people's novels isn't an acceptable short-cut; it's just a lazy road to disaster.)

Another reason why research is important is that it'll help to prevent you from telling the same story others have told before, even when you're covering well-trod ground. One of the reasons why *Ship Breaker* stands head and shoulders above so many other dystopian YA novels is because Bacigalupi obviously looked long and hard at the possible outcomes of global climate change and a post-petroleum future; his efforts show in every page. This is why I say that slipshod research and thematic clichés are really two sides of the same problem; if you attack the first aspect, then the second will take care of itself, because you'll find opportunities to do something original.

Second, use what you've learned to build your story. This is why it's important to do the bulk of your research *before* you start writing; the things you've learn will help you create the story itself, and also prevent you from having to drastically rewrite chapters when you later discover material that undermines the plot (or worse, struggle to justify something that's flat-out impossible, which like trying to pound a square peg into a round hole). Incorporate every bit of information you've learned when it's pertinent to your story; your notebook should be open in front of you while you write, and you should be checking at it often. I usually write four or five pages a day, but I know when I'm hitting the technical material when I'm barely able to get through three.

Third—and in some ways this is the most critical step—you reduce that material during the rewrite stage. All that stuff you've put in can be boiled down to the bare essentials by asking yourself two questions: *Does the reader really need to know this?* and *Does it help move the story along?* Sometimes a first-reader or an editor can help you judge what belongs and what doesn't, but it's really your job to make that determination yourself.

There's an art to depicting scientific and technological information in a novel so that it won't confuse or bore the reader. An old journalism professor of mine once gave me a nice pearl of wisdom: "It's not enough to write to be understood ...you must also write so that you can't possibly be misunderstood." If you use technical jargon, then you shouldn't count on your reader knowing what you mean. However, because long explanations are likely to elicit a yawn, definitions should be kept short. This is where the "show, don't tell" rule comes into play; the most elegant way of explaining something is to show it actually being used.

On the other hand, there are times when longer explanations are necessary: scene-setting, for instance, or descriptions of advanced technology. In those instances, you need to decide how much the reader needs to know in order for them to understand what's going on, and then boil it down to a paragraph or two, no more than three. It's okay to pause the action for something like this...so long as the explanation is kept short and sweet, and it's absolutely vital that the reader gains an understanding of the place or thing you're showing them.

One common misinterpretation of science fiction in general, and young-adult SF in particular, is that its main purpose is to teach science. This is Hugo Gernsbeck's definition of "scientifiction," but it's worth noting that Gernsbeck lost control of his own creation, *Amazing Stories*, when his business partners bought out what had become a failing magazine. No wonder that happened; many of the stories in early issues of *Amazing* were boring as hell, with the action suddenly coming to a screeching halt so that the writer could deliver a long, detailed lecture on a certain theory or invention, complete with mathematical equations. An effective SF story isn't a research paper in disguise; it's a story that uses science as its principal background. If you can inspire a reader to become interested in a given subject, that's great …but you're writing science *fiction*, not a textbook

Write the novel, and then mercilessly edit what you've written. It's a long and difficult process, but you'll get a better book out of it.

As in anything worth doing, it pays to study the masters.

Robert A. Heinlein's YA novels are often cited as the best examples of science fiction written for teenagers, and there's reasons why most of those books are still in print 60 years after they were written. Some like *Rocket Ship Galileo* and *Space Cadet* are now badly dated, but many of the others— *Time for the Stars*, *Tunnel in the Sky*, and *Citizen of the Galaxy* among them—hold up to this day. They should be read by anyone wanting to write young-adult SF as examples of how to do it right.

Yet Heinlein wasn't the only SF author who wrote well for a younger audience. During the 50s—the period that author and critic Barry Malzberg cites as being the genre's most formative era—quite a bit of YA science fiction was being published. Many of these books belonged to the highly-lauded Winston Science Fiction Series. Noteworthy titles include Arthur C. Clarke's *Islands in the Sky* (although it occasionally has the problems of technological overexposition I addressed earlier), *Vandals of the Void* by Jack Vance, *Vault of the Ages* by Poul Anderson (possibly the first dystopian YA novel) and *Danger: Dinosaurs!* by Richard Marsten (the pseudonym of Evan Hunter, aka Ed McBain).

Yet it was Lester del Rey (who, along with his wife Judy-Lynn del Rey, would later establish Ballantine's Del Rey Books SF imprint) who may have had the greatest impact among the Winston SF writers. Del Rey published a long parade of novels in this series, both under his own name and pseudonyms Erik Van Lhin and Philip St. John. Like Heinlein, his YA novels were thoroughly grounded in science and technology; the best include *Attack from Atlantis* (his use of Atlantis as a setting is forgivable; the other undersea material is near-perfect), *Marooned on Mars*, and the trilogy *Step to the Stars*, *Mission to the Moon*, and *Moon of Mutiny*.

Incidentally, one of Del Rey's YA novels, *Rocket Jockey* (originally published under the Philip St. John pseudonym) has an opening line which comes quite close to being a bona fide prophecy: "When Major Armstrong landed on the moon in 1964, his first words over the radar to Earth were: 'Who won the Indianapolis Classic?'" Del Rey deleted this line in later reprints of this novel that appeared under his own name, but he shouldn't have; he got right the last name of the first man to set foot on the Moon, and came within five years of pegging the date as well. Not bad for a book published in 1952.

Unfortunately, the Winston novels are out of print and hard to find, and usually expensive when they can be found. Very few had mass-market paperback reprints. If you can locate them in a library or borrow them from a friend, though, they're worth reading.

Andre Norton (the pseudonym, and later legal name, of Mary Alice Norton) was probably the most prolific YA writer in fantastic literature. Her later novels were almost all fantasy, but her early YA science fiction novels are classics. There's too many to list, but I recommend *Daybreak - 2250 A.D.*, *Star Born*, *Storm Over Warlock*, and her time travel/space travel series *The Time Traders*, *Galactic Derelict*, *The Defiant Agents*, and *Key Out Of Time* as great examples of how to write SF for teenagers.

Another classic YA science fiction novel is *Time of the Great Freeze* by Robert Silverberg, published in 1964 and reprinted in paperback several times since. This is one of Silverberg's lesser-known books but it holds up well to this day, particularly since it depicts a world suffering from the long-term consequences of global climate change, making it a novel well ahead of its time.

Alexei Panshin's *Rite of Passage* isn't usually regarded as a YA novel, mainly because of its sexual content (although this would be considered tame by contemporary standards). Yet it's a coming of age story set aboard a generation starship which bears Heinlein's influence while standing on its own. It won the Nebula Award for Best Novel when it was published in 1968 and has been reprinted many times since then.

Jupiter Project was Gregory Benford's first novel when it was published in 1975, and it too shows the Heinlein influence. It's worth reading because it shows how to wrap hard science into a fast-moving story.

Sadly, almost every example I've given here is currently out of print. You'll have to haunt second-hand bookstores or use online services like Amazon or ABE to locate copies; some are available as ebooks. These are the novels I read or re-read while I was gearing up to write my own YA novel, and I learned much from studying them.

Earlier in this essay, I criticized *The Hunger Games* for its thin scientific and technological underpinning. In the book's defense, some might point to the millions of copies sold and say that it doesn't matter. And in the most commercial sense, they'd be right. The author can point to her royalty statements, and it would be difficult for me to argue with her if she thumbed her nose at my objections.

On the other hand, there's a reason why it's necessary—even imperative—that authors of young adult SF make the effort to do their research and get the material right, and it is this: they're writing for teenagers.

It's hardly a revelation that science education in this country is at an all-time low. This has been the subject of newspaper articles for quite a while now; the statistics speak for themselves. At the same time, though, we're living in an age where knowledge of scientific and technological issues is more crucial than ever. Kids need to know more than just how to send text messages, but many schools aren't teaching them these things…often for reasons which have nothing to do with the schools themselves.

While it's not the job of science fiction to provide that education, what it can do is inspire kids to become curious about science and seek this knowledge for themselves. An entire generation got the urge to become involved in space exploration, in large part, by science fiction, whether it be Heinlein juveniles or *Tom Corbett, Space Cadet* (or, a few years later, *Star Trek*). Dystopian fiction can have a positive effect if it presents worst-case scenarios that teenagers may want to try to avoid, but there must also be visions of the future that tell us that civilization is not necessarily predestined for ruin and decay.

Young adult SF can be a force for change, if writers care to pursue this path. Editors, too, must need to see that there's greater purpose than chasing the bestseller list by pumping out redundant imitations of what's already popular. Innovation comes from taking risks, not just repeating prior successes… and there's an entire universe that hasn't yet been explored.

Those stories are out there, just waiting to be told.

CHAPTER 5

More Than Girl And Boy Books: Gender In YA

Leah Bobet

So guys, I wrote this sentence the other night.

"I reached up obligingly and took the heavy book like—" and I stopped. Because my instinct was to fill that blank in with *a baby*, and there was no reason this character, a sixteen-year-old girl with nobody she knows in diapers, a book of magic in her hands, and a lot of trouble ahead of her should go straight to thinking about babies. I wanted something heavy and dangerously delicate: Why not use an angry cat, or a fishbowl full of battery acid? I mean…*what?*

Which is when I clued in: It wasn't my writerbrain talking when I put that on the page. It was an old, stubborn, stupid bias.

(So. Sentence deleted. Try again.)

We're a little weird about biases right now: We all have them, because we all grew up in a society—and so have ideas about what people we know, or don't, are like—but we also know that having them isn't a good thing, and so we try not to admit it too loud. But one of the ways that learning to write well and honestly is kind of hard on a person is that it's a deliberate act: Learning to write is all about the thousand tiny choices we make when we join each word to the last one. And so writing forces you to look at yourself and the things you think, wherever they came from, and make sure each word really *is* a choice and not just a knee-jerk reaction. That nothing gets in the way of what you want to communicate to your readers, including your own ingrained assumptions.

How we talk about the people in our stories is one of those choices, and that's what we're about to kick around in the following pages: Making thoughtful choices when it comes to gender, stereotypes, boys, girls, trans*, genderfluid, and intersex characters, and who wears pink after all.

In other words: We're going to have a chat about YA novels, characterization, and gender.

Your Shortest Primer on Gender Ever
(So We Know What We're Talking About, and What We're Not)

So, in five seconds flat: *Gender? What you say?*

This is tricky, because there are a lot of things gender gets lumped in with or confused for that it actually has nothing to do with. For example:

Gender isn't about what parts are between your legs, when you're born or afterwards: that's your biological sex.

It's also not about who you like to make out with in dark corners, or whether you want to make out with anyone at all. That's your sexuality, and writing sexuality well is a whole other essay for a whole other day.

Gender is also—and this is a big one—not about your politics, and it's not code for feminism or "girl stuff." Regardless of your personal ideas on how the world should be run, or how you feel about how men and women treat each other, chances are you're expected to do or feel certain things just...because. You're a guy, so of course you like blue or red and not pink or pastels. You're a girl, so of course you'd rather watch romance movies than monster truck rallies. No one's asking what *you* want; it's just assumed. And there don't seem to be any real *reasons* behind what you can like and not like that go past just...because.

And that's what gender is: How our society divides people into categories—mostly the two favourites, boys and girls—and what we don't even ask about based on what you look like and what's between your legs. It's how we Act Like A Boy, or Act Like A Girl—and how we decide when how a boy or girl acts is *normal*.

Which is where we, as people, can kind of get into trouble. Because when we take it as fact that All Men don't like to be asked out by women, or always want to be the one who proposes marriage, or don't talk about their feelings; or All Women care more about emotions than sex, or will just quit that job anyway because a family is more important, it changes how we act toward each other. We start talking to, and about, these cardboard-cutout ideas of people instead of to the real person, and there's less and less room for us to just...act like not Boys or Girls, but like ourselves.

And it's where we can get into trouble as writers, too, because writing people who Act Like Boys or Act Like Girls takes away a lot of room to write characters who are three-dimensional; who leap off the page and make readers love or hate them. Because the thing is: Real people are just so much more *complicated*.

Whatever story you're telling—and this works across genre, age bracket, language, and even your reason for writing in the first place—one of the best tools in your toolbox for capturing a reader's imagination is to write really vibrant characters. Books like Rainbow Rowell's *Eleanor and Park*, John Green's *The Fault in Our Stars,* Rachel Hartman's *Seraphina*, and yes, Suzanne Collins's *The Hunger Games* all have nothing to do, really, with gender, but they all were absolutely loved, because the characters in them weren't concerned with doing Girl Things or Boy Things. Eleanor and Park start their friendship—and then romance—over music and comics. John Green's Hazel and Gus are too busy working through their cancer diagnoses and talking like hilarious, warm, nobody-else-is-you people to worry about how they look doing it. Seraphina has an identity to hide, and both men and women share her love of music—and I can go on.

All these books work because they show *people*, dealing with whatever situation they're in, in all their complicated, authentic glory. Not acting like the Gender Police are watching, but being utterly, entirely themselves.

This doesn't mean making rules against girls who like pink, boys who like steak and beer—or anything else. It means thinking, when we write a character, *is this action true to that person? Is it consistent with the rest of who they are?* It means building real people into our work: Not assuming things about what's normal, but focusing on what's *them*, no matter if they're a protagonist or on the page for five seconds flat.

Basically, it means no shortcuts. Sorry, guys.

(See? I did it again.)

But Wait, There's More!

There's a second thing to consider when it comes to writing characters with gender in mind: Just because we, society, like to divide people into girls and boys, it doesn't mean everyone's a girl or a boy. And there are a few more broad categorizations of people that we should be paying attention to.

In the same way we said that biological sex is the thing you call describing what's between your legs, intersex people are born with anatomy or genetics that make it not as easy to assign them as male or female. According to the Intersex Society of North America, one or two out of every 1,500 people have anatomy that's intersex—so that's a lot—but even though a few recent YA titles feature intersex characters, such as I.W. Gregorio's *None of the Above*, Abigail Tarttelin's *Golden Boy*, or Laura Lam's *Pantomime*, there aren't many books out there with intersex characters in any role.

There are a few more books, although still not enough, about transgender characters: People whose gender—their behavior and internal sense of being male, female, or neither—doesn't match their biological sex, regardless of whether they've had surgery or taken hormones to change that. *Beautiful Music for Ugly Children* by Kirstin Cronn-Mills and *Beauty Queens* by Libba Bray are both recent titles that have been praised for treating transgender characters well, and depicting them in a well-rounded way.

Nongendered or agender people are people who, like the prefix says, don't internally have a gender at all. There are not at all a lot of books that tackle this. David Levithan's *Every Day*'s protagonist jumps from body to body every morning, living a day of different people's lives—which can be taken as not having a gender per se. However, books that portray characters who just don't identify with gender and are standard-issue humans, living life, are not common in YA.

Genderfluid is a term that describes people who, like transpeople, don't feel that their internal sense of gender and behavior match their biological sex, but that's because their internal sense of gender is a moving target: it fluctuates rather than being one thing all the time. This is another experience I don't think I've seen yet in a YA novel. (Perhaps it could be yours!)

Notice how many of those ways of doing gender don't really appear in YA novels that much—and when they do, it's a big deal. There are reasons for this, and while some of them are unfortunately business-oriented and some come out of the same issues any representation of a minority will face, there is one that's right in our faces as authors.

It's important, when writing non-binary gender, to do it *really thoughtfully.*

Working with a character who doesn't fit neatly into the girl or boy boxes can be, unfortunately, extra hard if you're not living it, or close with somebody who is. There aren't enough stories by half out there that include trans*, intersex, or gender-fluid characters in any way, and while that means there's more room for yours, it also means that every way characters who aren't just *girls* or *boys* are portrayed becomes incredibly important to the real people who live those lives. It's fifteen times as important to question our own assumptions when writing these people and stories if they're not you or your stories, because readers with non-binary genders can't just fall back on the twenty books that got their life right when one does it poorly. There aren't twenty other books, and the feeling of *this is what people think I am* has that much more chance to hurt.

Think about every story about a trans*, or intersex, agender or genderfluid character as an advertisement saying something about *all* the trans*, intersex, or genderfluid people in the world. If a writer isn't careful about that advertising, it can end up being an attack ad. Yes, this sucks. But it is what happens when whole parts of the world walk into a bookstore and don't see much of themselves there, and the easiest way to make that better is to have more stories and viewpoints on those characters.

Basically, the easiest way to make that better is to go out and write those books *smart*.

There is no officially-stamped right way to do this, but I can offer a few pointers based on trying, talking to people, listening, and flat-out screwing up:

It's very important to remember, if you're not trans*, intersex, or genderfluid but writing that person as a character, that the first rule of character writing always applies: People are people, and people are complicated. (If you are writing non-binary characters as a non-binary author: Awesome! Keep it up! And you can probably skip this bit.) Transpeople don't sit around thinking about how transthey are all the time, just like Jewish people don't exactly spend every second on how different they are from Christians, Buddhists, and Muslims. One of the big pitfalls, if you're not writing from experience, in writing across social lines is treating the thing that makes a character different from *you* as the defining fact of that character's existence—when the most important thing about that person on that day might be getting a drummer for the band they're putting together, or the college application they just sent off, or how they'll get their homework done *and* babysit their kid brother so their single parent can work late. Or, y'know, where their morning coffee went for the love of God. People are people; and people have lives. All our ideas of *normal* are just based in the lives we live. It's when a writer treats someone different like not-people, or not-normal from their own perspective that a book is on shaky ground.

The second thing to pay strong attention to here is how trans*, intersex, or genderfluid characters are usually treated in books, movies, games, and TV. Writing's a conversation of sorts, where every book we write is read by readers in the context of all the *other* books. This leads to the situation where you think you're doing something totally respectful and original, and suddenly you've stepped in the dropped poop of a really pernicious stereotype you didn't even realize was there because you weren't looking at all the other books.

There are some pretty standard examples of these fictional stereotypes: The old black character always helps the young white protagonist gain folksy wisdom, and then conveniently dies. There is one girl character on the team, and her job is to fight the one girl villain. All transpeople want to have surgery to change their physical appearance. Transpeople in stories are almost always transitioning from male to female. Transpeople are violent or sexual predators who will corner you in the ladies' bathroom because they got surgery so they could come in. Basically, if it's on TVTropes, proceed with extreme caution.

These clichés might sound overblown if you're not familiar with them, and it shouldn't need to be said that they're all nothing like actual people are, but as stereotyped fictional characters, they just keep on going—and they're important to be aware of when you sit down to write non-binary characters.

Why? Well, because this isn't a hypothetical situation.

A few years ago I wrote a story which I thought commented in a very solid, empathetic way about how transpeople are people, and our cultural fixation with other people's bodies, and how it can drive someone off the rails to tell them they don't get to be themselves. The problem is: It was a murder mystery, because the series it was part of is a police procedural crime drama. And what I neglected to pay attention to is that transpeople get murdered at staggeringly huge rates in real life, and in real life their killers are usually not other transpeople, and so making a fictional world where a transperson killed others for having what other people wouldn't let her get was staggeringly hurtful in a few ways—it bought into stereotypes

I didn't even know existed, and covered over the real reasons real people get killed.

Hurting people with my work felt really, really bad—and this hurt real people, some of whom I consider friends. This all could have been solved with a little background reading, asking questions, doing research, and just…not assuming I knew everything there was to know about the subject. I didn't know there was anything there to see, really. But that's why I should have asked.

Learn from my mess-ups! Write non-binary characters; put them out there in your fiction. But make sure you do your homework and do it well.

So How Does This All Work in YA?

With all that background firmly chewed and swallowed? It depends.

The young adult section is a big place, and just like in a big city or country, what people assume about gender roles in YA depends on where you hang out. In certain subgenres, such as paranormal romance and dystopias, what boys do and what girls do has a pretty strict set of rules. For example:

Dystopian girls tend to the Sensitive But Tough, but still fall into nurturing caretaking roles—doing it all for someone else—given half a chance: Katniss of *The Hunger Games* goes into the games to spare her sister Prim; Ember of Kristen Simmons's *Article 5* is on the run to save her mother and the boy she loves; the otherwise harsh Saba of Moira Young's *Blood Red Road* goes into peril to rescue her twin brother. There's a delicate balance between doing for yourself and staying sympathetic by doing for someone else, to not cut the character off from the rest of the world.

Whereas in paranormal fiction, girls often fall into the box of Plucky, Vulnerable, But Special, and are frequently focused explicitly on what's outward: on the lookout for a boy who's stronger than them or can explain, respect, or contain their superpower. Boyfriends are werewolves, vampires, Shadowhunters, angels, wizards, or they go straight home with no goodnight kiss. There's a strong focus on dating, and making sure you date up: Obvious examples include *Twilight,* and Laini Taylor's *Daughter of Smoke and Bone.*

In other subgenres, like horror, epic fantasy, and contemporary, the field's a bit wider—and it's entirely probable that's because these are the subgenres that haven't had, or are just starting to have, major worldwide hits yet, and so people don't come to them looking for a book just like that last one. But that means how gender works in YA can be all over the map. You can have books that deal explicitly with gender roles and expectations—like Adrienne Kress's *The Friday Society,* which casts three young 19th-century women as perpetual assistants to the powerful (male) geniuses of Steampunk London, and then throws in a murder they themselves can solve to explicitly comment on what's expected of a lady while still being kind of goofily adventurous, fun, and hilarious; or Patrick Ness's *The Knife of Never Letting Go,* which is a frankly amazing punch in the stomach of a novel, mostly about a teenage boy working to figure out for *himself* what it means to be a man while on the run from his all-male hometown—on the shelf right next to novels where boys' job is to flex and brood, and girls' is to faint appropriately and present themselves for rescuing.

All this to say: There is a lot of room to do the things you want to do in YA, when it comes to gender roles. But there are still definite ideas of what a strong female protagonist, a proper boyfriend, or a boy who has adventures is in the age bracket, and these in-genre expectations can be just as much a straitjacket as any other gender stereotype. Whether you agree with them or want to undermine them, it's important to know they exist and to reply to them, rather than ignoring them.

This is one of the reasons that *read widely in the genre you're writing in* is such popular writing advice. It means you're getting the lay of the land and what readers of the kind of book you write expect people to be. You can find out what you love, what's been done, and what you want to agree or argue with.

The second factor to keep in mind in terms of writing gender well in YA is, unsurprisingly enough, age. If you're a teen or early-twenties writer, working on young adult books—well, good job! You probably know all the stuff I'm about to recommend, so just keep on with your bad self! But if you're an adult—even if you're a parent of teens—consider carefully that what you remember as "normal" high school age gender standards and behaviour have likely changed while you weren't looking, and that your perspective on them now is going to be very different from how it was at fifteen or seventeen.

Case in point: While promoting *Above*, I did a school visit in a small half-rural, half-military town high school, and was (pleasantly!) shocked at how unselfconsciously the boy students there showed each other fondness and affection. It was a thing that wasn't part of my teen years or my high school experience: I was much more used to the backpunching-means-I-love-you-because-boys-don't-hug way of doing business. And, well: I wouldn't have realized things had changed unless I'd gone and looked at it myself.

Age groups are subcultures like any other—ones that work differently in small towns, big cities, and parts of the world—and what my school visit experience proved was that if you want to know about how teen readers do gender, you have to go where they are. Does your library have a teen reading group, or is there a youth organization in your area? Go ahead and put in some solid volunteer hours. Aside from doing some good in your community and making some new friends, you'll learn more about what it's like to be a young adult in the place you live, and how the people you'll be speaking to with your work actually treat and think about things like gender; how they speak and act to each other.

Not everyone has the money, time, and wherewithal to volunteer, so there's another great resource to consider: talk to librarians, who know basically everything about what teen readers love, and where the conversation that is YA fiction is on certain topics. If there are teen readers in your life who will see it as a chance to be heard and not an imposition, talk to them! Ask them what fits and what doesn't fit in your work, and what you've been taking for granted.

Through all this, make sure you're listening more than you speak. These are mostly spaces to observe, hear, and learn, and your learning time—and other people's teaching time—is something to never waste.

So, How Do We Do This Thoughtful Gender Thing?
(Or: A Few Tests to Run On Your Own)

Down to the practicals: How do we know if we're writing gender thoughtfully and three-dimensionally, and not just setting ourselves up for *yet another* revision? Here are a few quick tests you can run to see if you have a gender stereotype issue on your hands.

- The Mad Libs Test: Switch your character from male to female. How does that thing they just said or did sound now? If it's perfectly normal in one gender, but sticks out as weird or wrong in another, then make sure you have a good reason for including it aside from "Of course that's how girls/boys think/act/speak!"

♦ Do a quick count: How many girls or boys do you have in your manuscript? If there's a good reason for that, like you're writing a story about a boy whose lifelong ambition is to join a nunnery and he has *just gone undercover*, well. That's probably cool, and I would like to read your book a lot. But otherwise, everyday life is a pretty mixed-gender place. Make sure your stories look like life, in that there are different kinds of people woven through it, and not just token women, men, or trans*, genderfluid, and intersex people.

♦ Once you've done your count and there's a healthy mix of genders in your work? Pat yourself on the back, first off, but then look at what those people's roles are in your story. Are the girls all somebody's girlfriend? Are the boys all potential love interests? If so, there's more work to do: Those are the shortcut places to include token girl or boy characters, the places we expect to see a man or a woman—the one love interest in an otherwise male or female world.

♦ Okay, we've got the more-than-love-interests covered. Check again: Are your girls all teachers, moms, waitresses? Are your boys all coaches, handymen, dads? If so, there's another layer of box to think outside of: the one where girls can do stereotypically boy jobs, and boys can do stereotypically girl jobs, and non-binary-gendered people can really do all those jobs as well—and that tends to make your work more *interesting*. Try making that sports-obsessed best friend a girls' varsity athlete, not a boys', like in Kendare Blake's *Antigoddess*; or that home ec teacher or stay-at-home parent a man, as in Sarah Rees Brennan's *Unspoken*. If that feels a bit weird in your head, that's not necessarily a bad thing: It means you're creating a character who's a person with a backstory and a life, not a shortcut or a placeholder for an archetype you haven't quite fleshed out. And it makes your whole fictional world feel more real.

◆   Try the Bechdel Test: Named after the cartoonist Alison Bechdel, this is basically asking yourself *Do I have at least two women in this story, who talk to each other about something other than a man?* If you're writing a work that's full of female characters (and it's not the aforementioned awesome nunnery book which, incidentally, I would really love to read), do you have at least two men talking to each other about something other than a woman?

◆   Can you sum up your secondary characters as The _____ Girl or The _____ Boy? Which is to say: The Pretty Girl; The Nerdy Boy; The Goth Girl; The Hot Boy. If so, you may want to take a second look at that. A character who can be summed up as The Nerdy Boy isn't being fully *himself*, fully three-dimensional; he's fitting closely into a stereotype and working as a shortcut. A big part of doing gender well in fiction is doing characters well, and shortcuts like this have a bad habit of being just bucketing with gender assumptions.

♦ Make mistakes, and then learn from them. There's no way in the world we're not going to put our foot in it sometimes, and that's kind of for the best: That is how people learn to do better, because if they're not messing up here and there, that means they haven't gone out of their comfort zone to *try*. But when you do make mistakes, make sure you don't make the same ones twice; be open-minded, be always learning, and always work on your craft.

Let's Sum Up, Team!

The challenge of writing YA books where we write gender smart, no matter whether it's with male, female, genderfluid, trans*, or intersex characters, isn't a small one—but it's one we can work at mostly by paying attention. And it's worth paying attention to: Not just because YA work sets, sometimes, an example, but because it means writing funny, smart, quirky, interesting, idiosyncratic, real, human, deliciously tangible people. The kind of people a reader can fall in love with—or just fall in love with the idea of wringing their neck into a paste.

It means not writing Girl Books or Boy Books but books, full stop, thereby doubling your audience (ha-ha, see what I did there?) and it means understanding our own heads and worlds, so that what we put in our books are the things we choose.

What did that mean for me the other night? It meant I spent half an hour on my stupid baby simile, because even though that story wasn't about gender roles, younger readers are pretty sharp customers. They understand that we say things about how the world works—and *can* work—not just in the Issue Books, but in what we casually assume is The Way the World Works in every story we put to paper. I was going to be saying something there about the world and girls' priorities and options, and it wasn't a thing I was sure I wanted to say.

That meant demanding of myself a better simile; to create better work. Even if it took half an hour.

Pay attention to the world, and always demand of yourself a better simile.

Good talk, everyone. Let's hit the non-gender-specific, individualized, three-dimensional, well-written showers.

CHAPTER 6

Creepy Or Romantic

Fanny Valentine Darling

I play a game with my daughter. It goes something like this:

Me: A boy you just met tells you that he is a monster, and in order to be with him you have to be his kind of monster. And in order to be his kind of monster, you have to literally die to join him. You've known him a month. You have to *die* to be his girlfriend. Die. You tell him to make you a monster, too.

Creepy or romantic?[1]

Her: Muh-ther! (Eyes roll.)

Me: Well?

Her: Creepy.

---

1   *Twilight* by Stephenie Meyer (Bella and Edward)

Or sometimes it goes like this:

> Me: Your parents have died, your family home is in danger, you decide to enter a dangerous horse race to try and keep your home and family together. You decide. While training for this race another competitor, who is favored to win, notices you have untapped skill and bravery, and also that you love horses. He begins to train with you, help you learn the ropes. He does not offer to throw the race for you, and he does not try to stop you from competing because it is "too dangerous."

Creepy or romantic?[2]

> Her: I love that book.

> Me: Answer please.

> Her: Romantic.

To be fair, I have read both of these books. Many times. So has my daughter. My fifteen-year-old self loves them both. My, ahem, older self, has serious issues with one of them. My mother self does not want my own fifteen-year-old daughter (when she gets there) to blindly believe that anytime a boy makes goo-goo eyes at you, and you swoon when he kisses you, that it's true love. And even if it *is* true love, that doesn't mean you lose yourself to that love. And, finally, my author self, my YA author self, believes that if I write the tales that make the Young Adult world read, I have some responsibility to show (not tell, not preach, not wag my finger and moralize) strong characters making strong choices. To be realistic in the message that *everything costs.*

In reality, my mother self guides most everything I do, even how I write. Because when I read a book now, I have to think

---

2 *The Scorpio Races* by Maggie Stiefvater (Puck and Sean Kendrick)

about whether or not it is a book I would feel comfortable letting my daughter read. This decision is not so much based on whether a book has themes or language that may be considered above her age range, but whether these themes are presented in a way that would make me feel the need to play a game of "creepy or romantic" with her while she read it.

So, do I believe YA authors have a responsibility to always tell the moral message?

No. Every YA book need not be "tonight on a very special episode of *Blossom*." In fact, part of what is so exciting about modern young adult literature is that it is *not* written to cater to parents who want to "teach" to our children, but it is written to entertain them, to get them excited about a life as a reader. One of the wonderful things about watching my daughter read is when sometimes she finds "the" book, the one that makes her read at the dinner table, stay up later than she should for one more chapter, and talk about the characters as if they are friends. When I was my daughter's age, I had Judy Blume, who I loved, but who was very "message" centric; and Lois Duncan, who launched my love of the paranormal. And lots of middle-grade After School Special type books. Most of them were well written. But I read the cover off my copy of *The Third Eye* by Lois Duncan. I think I still know many passages by heart. In that book, there were some morally questionable themes. And some frightening (to parents) ideas and scenes. A child's kidnapping, the main character's feeling of guilt about the kidnapping, her fear of her psychic ability, and her crush on the older (by about four to six years, if I remember correctly) police officer handling the case. Duncan didn't tell me this crush was wrong. She showed it honestly but appropriately, allowing both characters to feel the chemistry, and hinting at a future relationship when it would be acceptable.

Characters become our friends. Young adults listen to their friends, so as a parent, I want to meet her friends, introduce her to ones that I think say something interesting, or intelligent, or funny. Sometimes those friends will make a choice I find to be questionable. I have never told my daughter she was not allowed to read a book. I don't believe in that, personally, but I understand that every parent is not going to agree with me.

When I was ten years old, and my older sister was twelve, in the summers I went to visit my father. He was a Methodist minister, and had been assigned to a church in Oklahoma, in a small town that still had wooden sidewalks and a general store with a dirt floor. The first thing my sister and I did upon arriving with the moving truck was run to the library. It was summer, and we had plans to lock ourselves in a room with the air conditioning blasting and read for the next nine weeks. Arms loaded with books, including *The Shining* and *The Amityville Horror*, we made our way to the check-out desk. The town knew who we were, of course: the preacher's kids. The librarian took one look at our selections and told us to hit the bricks. I had never in my life been told I couldn't read something. I wasn't so much angry as befuddled. My sister? She was angry. We returned to the parsonage and enlisted the help of my step-mother, who followed us back to the library, hair falling out of her moving bun and jeans shorts probably shorter than she would have liked for the town's first sighting of the preacher's wife. The stack of books was still sitting on the counter next to the disapproving librarian when we came level with her. My step-mother introduced herself, looked through the stack of books, and approved our selections. Not willing to say no to the new preacher's wife, the librarian checked the books out to my step-mother, who handed them over to us and we went home happy.

That day made a huge impact on me. I learned about my step-mother's respect for reading, and I learned that she trusted us to choose our own stories. (Though, if we'd woken her up at three in the morning because of a nightmare, I'm not sure her feelings about our mature reading levels would have been so solid.) And I learned that children self-censor. When I read *The Shining* again in my early 20s, I was shocked by what happened in room 237, and was sure I was reading a new expanded version of the book, because I knew, just knew I hadn't read that when I was ten. Both the scary and the sexy. I remembered none of it.

Language, sex, drugs, and rebellion are a part of entering young adulthood. I think most parents would agree. Therefore most authors listening to the honesty of their characters will incorporate some measure of rebellion. That rebellion can reveal itself in the form of foul language, sneaking out of the house, sneaking alcohol from the liquor cabinet, buying a dime bag from the local pothead, or going to third base with the cute boy around the corner. Or making the decision to do none of these things, but at the very least entertaining the concept of doing something that an authority figure did not and would not approve. As a parent, I think the first and easiest conclusion to jump to is: "I don't want my kid to do that. Therefore, I don't want my kid to read about kids who do that." I don't want my kid to sneak out of the house and taunt the local shut-in, so should I tell her not to read *To Kill a Mockingbird*?

Everything costs. Each choice leads to a reaction and a consequence—not necessarily a moral, but if teen behavior is to be true and real, and the result believable, writing about teens as teens includes their recklessness, their passion, and their belief that they very well might be immortal. Many young people think they live in a vacuum, and much young adult literature is about learning that they do not. Selfishness, rudeness, sass, and rebellion are natural traits of a teen. Jumping into the void of danger, excitement, and sex are intoxicating notions, too. As a parent, I prefer the first time my child explores these concepts to be in the pages of a book. A practice run, if you will.

Here's my take-away on the message books vs. the plot driven books: Young adults, much like their adult counterparts, know when they are being preached to—when a book is written merely to be a warning or a sermon. Telling a story about bullying needs to be about the characters, the plot, and then about the bullying. Including a rape in your story? It better have some reason to be there other than a convenient way to have your character saved by a white knight. Morality is not a plot device.

Further, when young adults are introduced to morally ambiguous plots and characters, they have the ability to decide how they feel about them. The world is a morally ambiguous place.

Now, having drawn a pretty wide line in the sand about messages and morals, I turn it all on its head when it comes to telling my child about what young love and a healthy teenage relationship looks like. I am still not going to tell my kid she can't read a book, but we are going to have some heavy conversations about:

Stalker vs. Hero

This is seems to be a particularly wavy line in YA when it comes to "he's so into me!" behavior. Boys who sneak into a girl's room to watch her sleep, boys who have decided which one of them a girl will date (without consulting the girl, of course), boys who have girls followed, listen in on phone conversations, read their diaries... This phenomenon seems to be particularly male-character specific. The idea that there's something romantic about following a girl without her knowledge or consent, or spying on her in her home or through her personal items, is frighteningly prevalent in YA. I can't think of a plot that includes a girl treating the object of her affections in a similar manner. This is not to say the girls aren't given their fair share of unhealthy romantic role models, but more on that later.

Creepy or romantic?

Boy breaks into girl's room without her knowledge or consent, to watch her sleep.[3]

Creepy or romantic?

Boy, who was not following girl, finds her injured (after she has fought off her attacker on her own). He helps her walk back to his house and tends to her wounds.[4]

Creepy or romantic?

Boy, who is a friend of girl's college roommate, knows that girl has been writing with a lab partner in the on-campus library until late at night, and said lab partner walks home in another direction. He requests girl call him when she leaves the library so he can walk her back to her dorm room safely.[5]

Controlling vs. Protective

This is another phenomenon generally ascribed to the fictional males in romantic relationships, though not *quite* as exclusively as the stalker theme. Both Tributes from District 12 are guilty of this behavior. I tell my own daughter, it is good to feel protective of what you love (your significant other, your family, your friends, your pets). It's fine to take actions in that direction. But when those actions include lying about or hiding facts from someone, deciding who they may or may not associate with when you are not around, insinuating yourself into their every waking moment, asserting your opinion of their treatment to someone you think has mistreated them

3 *Twilight* by Stephenie Meyer (Bella and Edward)
4 *Paper Valentine* by Brenna Yovanoff (Hannah and Finny)
5 *Fangirl* by Rainbow Rowell (Cather and Levi)

without their desire or consent...even if you're always picking up a sleeping pet for an unwanted cuddle instead of letting it sleep, you've crossed a line into controlling and unhealthy behavior.

Creepy or Romantic?

Boy, deciding that he is wrong for girl, and other boy is right for her, does not have conversation with girl about his feelings. Instead he invites her to his room and humiliates her to such a degree that she becomes so hurt, embarrassed, and angry as to be unable to make her own decision about continuing their relationship/friendship.[6]

Creepy or Romantic?

Boy finds out girl is in an unsafe home environment which has just crossed the line into a dangerous situation. After talking for hours, he drives her to a relative's house a couple of states away, even though he is aware it means she may never return to the town he lives, and could end their relationship.[7]

Love vs. Losing Yourself

As much as the stalker role seems reserved for the males of the young adult species, handing oneself over—mind, body and soul—is pretty much the domain of the female. In its extreme, Bella Swan from *Twilight* makes the decision to go into the woods with Edward Cullen even after he has admitted there is a very strong chance he may not be able to control his bloodlust, and could kill her. Kill her. Let me say that again, *kill her.* She goes with him anyway, because after three conversations with him, she knows she is so in love with him that if she can't be with him, it's better to allow him to drink her blood until she dies. *Dies.* Within a month, she is

---

6 *Clockwork Angel* by Cassandra Clare (Will and Tessa)
7 *Eleanor and Park* by Rainbow Rowell (Eleanor and Park)

begging Edward to change her into a vampire. In order to be turned into a vampire, you must die. After a month, she is sure that she is willing to die to be with the first boy she ever kissed, forever. As I counseled my daughter, the vast majority of people will not even fall in love with the first person they kiss, let alone spend all of eternity with them.

An alarming number of female characters in YA are so "in love" that they stop making decisions for themselves. They may see that their partner's behavior is alarming, but are either talked out of their concern by the boy's assertion that he loves her and only wants what is best for her, or they convince themselves that because his love is so strong, what he is asking or doing is somehow romantic. They do what the boy wants, think what the boy thinks, and turn to him for the decisions. They do not work as a team, they hand over their brains to "love."

I want my daughter to be kind to her boyfriends (or girlfriends, or whoever she ends up dating), to be thoughtful of their feelings, to share her dreams and her desires with them. I want her to think they hang the moon and the stars (and I want them to be worthy of those feelings, though I am sure some of them will not be). I want the stories that she reads about love to show how exciting it is, how all-encompassing it can feel, and ultimately that hanging on to your own sense of self in a relationship is the smartest and most exciting path.

Creepy or Romantic?

Your boyfriend has a lesser station in life than you, you do not care, you just want to be with him. However, he encourages you to try and improve your lot in life. By entering a contest to go to the palace of the prince and compete against thirty-four other girls to become the princess. Because you love your boyfriend so much, you agree that he must be right about this, and you enter the contest.[8]

---

8 *The Selection* by Kiera Cass (America and Aspen)

Creepy or Romantic?

Your boyfriend is a devil-may-care werewolf rockstar, with a rather large self-destructive streak. Although you would love to run away with him and pretend all the problems with your relationship just don't matter because you love him and love will win out, instead you decide to take some time for yourself and tell him you want him to work out his problems, and hopefully the two of you can work it out once he's matured.[9]

Sex vs. Rape (blurred lines? Unclear consent?)

"Because that's not love, Beth. That's rape."
—Stephen King, "I Know What You Need"

I read Stephen King's short story "I Know What You Need" when I was a teen. The story is about a psychic who woos a girl by using her unspoken desires and needs. Eventually it is discovered, and the girl still believes she is in love with him. Her friend points out that she can't believe what she feels for him because he was never honest with her. I remember being struck that there were different kinds of rape. I was young, and luckily had never encountered any kind of sexual pressure from my dates, so possibly I was naive. This was also before date rape was talked about in classrooms on a regular basis, and years before roofies. I never forgot that story, or that lesson. As a parent, I want the books my child reads to show appropriate sexual relationships, and if there are blurry lines, I want that to be a part of the story. I want someone to question inappropriate sexual behavior.

The decision to have sex does not have to be weighted to such an extreme that it becomes a life and death decision.

9 *Linger* by Maggie Stiefvater (Isabel and Cole)

Teenagers have sex. They do. Lots of them. Some of them do not. As a parent, I don't need to read pages and pages of "should we or shouldn't we" discussions, I don't need step by step consent between partners. But I *do* want to know that each person engaging in the act has made the decision to be there, doing what they are doing.

Creepy or Romantic?

Boy and girl have been dating for over a year, girl has been interested in making relationship a sexual one, boy is more experienced and he counsels restraint for many reasons. There is an open line of communication, and both boy and girl admit to feeling frustrated sometimes. When the time comes, the sex is sweet, and awkward, and full of many questions and obvious consent.[10]

Creepy or Romantic?

Girl, recently out of a traumatic experience finally finds herself in a place of safety. She attends a party. Girl gets very drunk. Boy, fully aware of girl's recent past, and her inebriated state encourages her to have sex with him.[11]

Healthy Growth vs. Insta-love

Young adult novels are shorter than adult novels. Teenagers experience things much more intensely than adults, with less hesitation and less fear. Fair enough. Relationships in young adult novels move at an accelerated pace. There is a certain understanding of that, and then there is the growing spread of insta-love in YA pairings. Boy meets girl. Boy takes girl out on date. Boy and girl declare undying love forever and ever. Can we please have at least three scenes of boy and girl learning a bit about each other? Some time to understand

---

10 *Carpe Corpus* by Rachel Caine (Claire and Shane)
11 *Darkness Be My Friend* by John Marsden (Ellie and Adam)

what has blossomed, some appreciation of how huge love is, how wonderful it feels to fall into love? The excitement of being on the cusp of love is so amazing, why are we so quick to skip over that step in our quest to be in love? I do not want my daughter to rush to the "goal" of being in love. If love alone is the goal, the person you are with becomes irrelevant. And that negates the purpose of being in love.

Creepy or Romantic?

Girl and boy have been paired on an undercover project to protect another. During this time they have lots of time to have long, involved chats about their likes and dislikes, their favorite books, future aspirations, and what they think of grass growing. They begin to discover a growing attraction to each other, and then realize that they have fallen in love.[12]

Creepy or Romantic?

Boy feels like he is an outsider in his small, southern town. All he wants in the world is to get out. He meets the new girl in town. He talks to new girl. He walks new girl home. He loves new girl, she's his destiny, it's fate.[13]

Happily Ever After When There Shouldn't Be? Now vs. Later

"And they lived happily ever after..." Happily ever after can and should mean many different things to young people. Without a very-far-in-the-future epilogue (*Mockingjay*, *Harry Potter and the Deathly Hallows*) I find it a little disconcerting when "happily ever after" automatically includes marriage and forever and ever. Again, it's an unrealistic expectation of teen love. The pressure to give teens their idealized vision of what true love's happy ending should be is intense. Much like

---

12 Bloodlines Series by Richelle Mead (Sydney and Adrian)
13 *Beautiful Creatures* by Margaret Stohl & Kami Garcia (Lena and Ethan)

insta-love, happily ever after models prioritize the goal over the journey. Being in a relationship that lasts forever becomes more important than living your life and experiencing the highs and lows of it with the one person you most want at your side.

Creepy or Romantic?

At the end of a long protracted war with bad vampires, two teenage couples have a double wedding.[14]

Creepy or Romantic?

After a long, protracted war to rid themselves of a werewolf virus, two young lovers start their life together as a dating couple, it may or may not last forever.[15]

Creepy or Romantic?

Girl genius (college at sixteen) moves to a town far from her parental home, is bullied at the dorms and moves into a house of slightly older misfits. While an attractive girl, she is not a bombshell, and pays more attention to her science book than her haircut. Boy roommate initially feels protective and a friendship develops. Once full extent of her intelligence and inner strength is discovered, boy realizes this is what has stoked the flames of attraction for her, and finds himself madly in love.[16]

In Summary

So, who's doing it right? I feel like I've pointed fingers at a lot of books that commit parental sins. I want to make clear: I do not condemn those books. I've only mentioned books I've personally truly enjoyed—even if, while I was reading them, my parental inner voice groaned and composed the next

---

14 *Daylighters* by Rachel Caine (Shane and Claire & Michael and Eve)
15 *Forever* by Maggie Stiefvater (Grace and Sam)
16 The Morganville Vampire Series by Rachel Caine (Shane and Claire)

conversation with my child. The author's choices, the choices I might have made if I had written the books, the choices she might have made if she was the main character...honestly, I *love* these conversations. And in the end, it is my job to parent. It's not the book's responsibility. On the other hand, those authors who nail it make me cheer, make my conversations with my child even more inspiring, and force me to reach further in my own writing for other people's children.

For some examples of authors who are showing what I've been telling, please see Appendix D.

CHAPTER 7

Making Your Readers
Team Players

Julie Kagawa

With the wild success of Stephenie Meyer's *Twilight Saga*, readers everywhere have gone team crazy. What started with "Team Edward" and "Team Jacob" has grown into one of the most common tropes in young adult literature, with authors and readers happy to go along for the ride. In this article, I will look at what makes the concept of teams so popular, and what aspiring authors should think about when trying to incorporate them into their words.

Teams: What's the Big Deal?

We all know that "teams" are popular. You can scarcely open a book or read a review without "Team Somebody" jumping out at you. But why is that? What makes us as readers so willing to divide the protagonists of a story into sides and pick one to relentlessly—almost savagely—root for? One of the simplest (and best) reasons is that any conflict automatically adds dramatic tension to a story, and teams, by their very nature, create conflict. Take a moment and think about your favorite team from any of the novels you have read. Now, try to imagine that same novel with the "other" team no longer present. Things just got a lot more dull, right? By introducing the rivalry and competition that is at the very heart of the "team" concept, the author is telling the reader that there is something at stake, something to be won, and, conversely, something to be *lost*. There is risk and reward, success and failure, winners and losers—and it is during these times, the high-stress, all-or-nothing, everything-on-the-line times— that the true hearts of the characters come out. What could be more tense, more dramatic, than that?

It's not all about winning and losing, though. Teams, particularly with regard to the love triangle, are also about making choices—and not just for the characters. In *The Iron Fey*, Meghan had a choice to make between Ash and Puck, and struggling with that choice, weighing her feelings and emotions, balancing her passion for the steely-eyed ice prince against her love for the friend that had always been there for her, provided some of the most dramatic and tense scenes in the series. Just like competition, *choice* helps build drama and make the story more real. Imagine a book where the protagonist doesn't have to make any choices, where she is simply swept along by events, with no power to affect things or have an impact on the world around her. Sounds pretty boring, right?

But the beautiful thing about teams is that it's not just about choices for the characters in the story. Teams break the fourth wall and draw the *reader* directly into the same choices that face the protagonist. Early in the 2000s this phenomenon wouldn't have been possible, but the explosion of social media has created a platform for readers to express their team choice to thousands (or tens of thousands, or millions!) of dedicated fans around the world. And not just express, but declare, debate, debunk, and defend, creating friendly rivalries that extend beyond the covers of the book and bring the same choices the protagonist faces into the real world.

Every story needs drama and tension and choice, excitement and adventure (and other things Jedi crave not). The best stories achieve these things on multiple levels—through the plotting, through the character development, in some cases even through the setting and the world itself. The "team" is another tool in the author's toolkit to bring these elements to the story and stretch them beyond into the real world as well.

Which all sounds great, of course. But *how* does one go about actually doing it?

Writing the Team

Okay, so now that we have a general idea of *why* we like teams, it's time to start looking at *how* you can go about introducing them into your own writings. But what makes teams, teams? What makes readers want to cheer for one side or another? And how do you weave teams into the story in such a way that you're not just putting in a team for the sake of having a team? In other words, how do you make them a meaningful and important part of the work?

A Note on Team Types

The most common team type in Young Adult fiction is probably the love triangle. Some of you who just read those words cringed a little. Others felt a thrill of excitement. The terrible trouble with tropes is that they can be overused or poorly implemented. On the other hand, tropes *become* tropes because people like them. It's kind of like vampires. Remember when people said vampire stories were on their way out? They still seem to be sticking around, though.

There is absolutely nothing wrong with the love triangle, and it's important to remember that it's been around a lot longer than young adult fiction. You could look to *Cyrano de Bergerac* (Rostand, Edmond, 1897) in the late 1800s or (my personal favorite) all the way back to *A Midsummer Night's Dream* by William Shakespeare, with a publication date believed to be somewhere in 90s… the 1590s. Both are famed for their love triangles, one tragic, the other comic. In both, the love triangles serve to do all the things I mentioned before—build dramatic (or comedic) tension, develop characters, and force choices.

While the love triangle is probably the most common situation that leads to the creation of "teams," it's important to remember that it doesn't have to be the *only* situation that does so. You might have a dedicated FBI agent trying to track down a charming but lonely criminal as in *Catch Me If You Can* (Spielberg, Steven, dir. Dreamworks SKG, 2002) or two brothers both invested in the world of mixed martial arts who are trying to win the same title, as in *Warrior* (O'Connor, Gavin, dir. Lionsgate, 2011). What matters is that you have two (or more) sides that are both *likable* and that have something at stake. I will speak more to the likeability of the characters as we go on. The important thing to remember is that "teams" can be born from more than the love triangle. That said, because I write what I write, most of my focus will lean more towards the love triangle as the most common trope for introducing "teams."

Building the Team

Enough of the theory and types and whys. It's time to get down to brass tacks. How do you actually go about building characters that lend themselves to creating "teams" among readers?

Separate and Distinct Teams

First, and this may sound obvious, but it's worth stating, you have to have separate and distinct sides. That doesn't mean that you throw a couple of dreamy boys in your protagonist's path and have her go all gooey for both of them. What's important here is the "separate and distinct" part. There has to be real and tangible differences between the two "sides" of the team—not just in their physical makeup, but deeper, into what makes the characters who they are. Their quintessential characteristics have to be not only different, but, ideally, polar opposites. Whatever choice the protagonist ultimately makes should be based on those characteristics and should inform on who the protagonist herself is.

Take *The Iron Fey*. Both Puck and Ash are fiercely loyal to Meghan. Both would do anything to help her and keep her safe. But that's how the two are *alike*...being the same doesn't exactly lend itself to having teams. What creates teams are those key aspects that separate Ash and Puck. Puck represents all that is mischievous, irreverent, and carefree. He thumbs his nose at authority, shirks responsibility, and lives by the notion that the point of life is to have a little fun. Ash, on the other hand, is stoic, responsible, determined. He's haunted by his past, which makes him melancholy and brooding. In short, in all the ways that really matter, he's the exact opposite of Puck.

When readers pick sides, when they declare for a "team," they tend to gravitate towards the characteristics that they themselves find most appealing. Do you prefer the witty smart-ass? Go Team Puck! Are you more into the brooding bad-boy? Go Team Ash. If both characters were haunted by their pasts, or if both were masters of sarcasm, there wouldn't be much choice between them. It would be like choosing between a peanut butter and strawberry jelly sandwich or a peanut butter and grape jelly sandwich—sure, there's a little bit of difference, but it's pretty much the same thing.

Likeable Teams

It is absolutely necessary that the characters you're building into your "teams" are separate and distinct from each other, but that alone is not enough to create a good team dynamic. In addition to being different, both "teams" also have to be *likeable*. In Harry Potter, you have Harry on one side, and Draco on the other. Both are very distinct from one another. You even have something for them to compete over (be it Quidditch or a House Cup). But even though you find people rooting for "Team Snape" or "Team Slytherin," it's in a very different context from what most consider "teams" in Young Adult Fiction. That's because through building Draco Malfoy and Slytherin, J.K. Rowling wasn't setting up a team... she was introducing antagonists and foils for Harry. Even though Draco and Snape were sympathetic in their own right (especially Snape, once you really understood him), they were there, as a whole, to make life difficult for the protagonist.

In order to introduce teams into your writing, your sides both need to be likeable. The reader needs a reason to root for either team, not just the team that you, as the author, know is going to win. This goes back to introducing a choice, both to your protagonist and to your readers. For that choice to be meaningful, it has to be hard, and let's face it, choosing between Prince Charming and a complete and total tool really isn't much of a choice. To paraphrase comedian Eddie Izzard, it becomes a "cake or death" situation. If you had to choose between cake and death, well, gee, I guess I'll have the cake.

In order to avoid this, you have to make sure that the team "players" are fully realized characters that the reader actually likes. Entire books can (and have) been written on making your characters likeable, so I won't delve too deeply into the mechanics of that. Just remember that for teams to be a meaningful part of your writing, there should not be a "right" team and a "wrong" team. Instead, you should strive create characters that present a real and meaningful choice to your protagonist.

But what's the point of that choice? And why does it matter? I'm glad you asked.

The Choice as Characterization

An important, and often overlooked, aspect of "teams" in fiction is that they can be a vital tool in building characters. We've already talked about the factions needing to be separate and distinct from one another, so there is some characterization baked into the creation of the players. That's all well and good, and can lead to the development of a wonderfully diverse cast to grace the pages of your writing, but there's another aspect of characterization that "teams" can drive, not for the members of the "teams" but for the protagonist and the reader. That is, of course, the choice.

We all make choices every day. Most are the little every day minutiae of choice that we don't really even think about. Do we have chicken or beef for dinner? Do we walk, or drive, or take the bus? You may not think these choices reveal a lot about a person's character, and in the real world, much of the time they don't. But they *absolutely can*. One of the wonderful things about writing is that it tends to be an exaggeration of reality. Not many books are written about people who get up, go to their jobs, live a mundane, workaday existence, and retire into anonymity. Books are all about excitement and drama and stress and tension. And choices totally drive (and derive) from these things.

A character's dinner choice might not seem like it can contain aspects of characterization, but what if the character chooses to only eat free-range chicken, because she deplores the conditions in which farm-raised chickens are kept? Or, what happens if the character always chooses to walk when possible because she believes that any little part she can do to keep the air cleaner is worth the effort? Suddenly, these choices start giving us insight into the character, into her morals and ethics, her beliefs, and what makes her tick. And these are the small, every-day choices that most of us don't even think about.

When you introduce the concept of teams, and, ultimately, a protagonist having to make a choice between those teams, the stakes get much, much higher. If we return to the example of Meghan, Puck, and Ash, we can look at what Meghan's choice (Warning: here there be spoilers!) ultimately says, not about Puck or Ash, but about Meghan herself. Over the story arc of *The Iron Fey*, Meghan goes from being your typical teen-aged outcast concerned about being popular and meeting boys and grows to become a powerful young woman who is willing to sacrifice everything for those she loves and those she comes to see as her people.

Given our earlier characterizations of Puck and Ash—Puck as the carefree prankster who shirks responsibility, and Ash as the dedicated stoic—which sounds more like the kind of person who would rise to rule a Court of the Fey, stand up against the Kings and Queens of Winter and Summer? Within the context of the plot, Meghan's choice of Ash is about finding true love. But from a characterization standpoint, Meghan's choice of the "team" that stands more for responsibility and sacrifice instead of the "team" that stands for the carefree unfettered spirit speaks to the fact that she has grown up over the course of the novels and learned to put others before herself and her own happiness. In her choice, we see that core aspects of her character have developed and changed, grown from who she was (when the choice was uncertain and she could have gone either way) into a person who Ash, and only Ash, could be the right choice for.

How Do You Choose?

As the writer of a work that includes teams, you will, ultimately, have to make a choice between them. But if we've created such likeable, distinct teams, how do we choose? The good news is, that while the choice should not be obvious to the reader at the outset of the story, by the time you get to the end of the tale, things should have cleared themselves up nicely. In short, since the choice your protagonist makes is quintessential to her characterization, the way that your character has grown and evolved should guide you to the "right" choice. No doubt some of your readers will disagree with you, or wish things had gone the other way, but that's part of the fun!

It is very important to remember to *make* that choice. Just as having an obvious choice at the *beginning* of the story can be problematic (cake or death!) having no clear choice by the *end* of the story causes just as many problems. If your protagonist hasn't grown or changed enough that she has a clear idea of what "team" she's on, you run the risk of having an indecisive, wishy-washy hero—something that no reader really enjoys. Worse, if the choice is made without any real change in the character to support it, it becomes a coin flip scenario... "Uhm, I'll be with (flips coin) Team Winner from now on! Yay!" This will likely result in your readers sharpening their pitchforks and oiling up their torches.

Putting It All Together

Teams have become an integral part of many Young Adult (and some Adult) works of fiction, and they're here to stay. And why not? They work to build drama and tension, and add another layer of excitement to your writing by instilling an almost immediate sense of competition. Unlike many literary devices used throughout the ages, they possess the ability to transcend the page and pull the readers directly into the heart of the story, giving them the power to make the choice for themselves and declare that choice to the world. As with all literary devices, they can be done well. Unfortunately, as with all other literary devices, they can also be overused, abused, and otherwise maligned. But if you keep a few key things in mind, you should be able to introduce a team mechanic into your writing that will not only get your readers taking sides, but will help to drive the characterization and plotting of your work.

Remember, your teams must be distinct and separate from one another, and these differences must be readily apparent to your readers. In addition, your teams have to be made up of characters that your readers will actually like and want to cheer for. Those two things will go a long way to presenting a real and difficult choice to your protagonists (and your readers) as they struggle with which team they're "on." And, perhaps most important, you have to make sure that whatever decision your protagonist makes, it is supported not only in the context of the plotting, but also becomes the natural end product of the way your characters have grown and changed throughout the course of your writing. Don't fall into either the "cake or death" or the "coin flip" trap.

If you follow these few simple guidelines, you will be able to build a solid framework from which to inject teams into your own works. So go forth, create teams, pick sides, argue and debate their merits, and most of all, keep writing!

CHAPTER 8

Trans 101 for YA Writers

Sassafras Lowrey

So you want to write about gender?

As a genderqueer author I often engage in conversations with other trans writers about the representation of gender variant characters within new literature. Increasingly their conversations have included representation within YA as more of us like myself found ourselves somewhat accidental YA authors, and others intentionally pursue YA literary careers with an interest in representing trans characters. I think that there is a lot of truth to the old writing adage that we should "write what we know." There is a lot of legitimacy to putting to the page the stories that we at least in part know through personal experience. However I don't think that is the only way to write a strong story, and it's not always possible for us to write books based on stories that are our own.

Especially within YA, if we are writing contemporary set novels, very few of us are presently teens and so even on that basic level we are adults writing stories and experiences that are not our own. More important to me than if someone is writing from personal experience/understanding about an issue is their reasoning behind the stories that they are writing. Write trans characters because trans people are part of our world, not because you think it's trendy or edgy.

There is an increased pressure for writers to critically engage with the diverse world around us, especially within YA. This is important because youth deserve well-written, complex and engaging books where they can see themselves and their communities reflected on the page. This Chapter is really an intro guide to set you on the right path to creating believable and culturally sensitive trans characters. This Chapter won't give you all the tools you need to go out and write a novel with a transgender protagonist—there is far more research you'll need to do—but it will set you on the right direction, and help you avoid some basic (and unfortunately common) transphobic pitfalls.

Just because you've seen a trans person in a movie, or been friends with one trans individual doesn't that you're ready to start including trans characters in your writing in a culturally competent way. Some good questions to be asking yourself set get of you wasn't to write trans characters? What does writing a trans character mean to you? In some ways writing a transgender character is like writing any other character, you need to start with character outlining and development so that when you are writing you can really be in their head and understand their motivations. When the character you are writing is of trans experience, you need to know why this character is trans, what being trans means to them, and how that does (or doesn't) influence the way that they interact with other characters in the book, and the environment you are writing around them. If a character isn't as three dimensional as the other characters around them, they will stand out as a token.

For trans people, gender identity/expression is one aspect of who we are. One mistake that many cisgender writers often make when writing trans characters is to write stories where a character's trans identity, and specifically a physical transition or coming out, is the focal point of the story. Coming out stories are important, but I implore you to think beyond the coming out narrative when you are creating YA literature with trans characters. Teens today are smart and engaged, they often have a more nuanced understanding of gender and sexuality than adults do, and they are hungry for more interesting stories that feature trans protagonists, but don't relegate them to a coming out storyline.

Glossary

Within YA writing there remains an ongoing debate around the importance and critique about authors writing about experiences that are not your own, especially when that experience is one that has been highly marginalized or oppressed in society, and the writer is coming from a position of privilege. Just like there are concerns/questions when white writers create stories about people of color, or men write stories about women, some transgender writers and activists raise eyebrows when cisgender writers create stories about GNC/transgender characters (are you understanding the words I'm using here? If not you are in the right place, this section is going to help you to get some of the language you'll need to start exploring writing transgender characters.

If you are a cisgender (someone who isn't trans) writer intending to write a novel featuring a trans writer one of your first jobs is going to be to understand how to talk about your gender nonconforming characters in ways that are accurate, and affirming.

One of the first things that will throw off the believability of your character is the use of outdated, or inaccurate language to describe gender identity or expression. In this section I provide a glossary of some of the more common terminology related to trans communities. The inherent trouble with creating a glossary of this nature is that terminology is continually shifting, growing and evolving. The language trans communities used ten years ago when I was coming out has shifted radically from the language that we use today. Additionally, there are as many definitions for some of these words as there are trans people, which leads to ongoing debates about definitions. With that disclaimer, the following are some common terms related to gender variance which will be useful to you both as you write, but also in your initial research phase.

Transgender 101 Glossary of Terms

- **GNC (GENDER NON CONFORMING)**: a term which refers to individuals whose identities or gender expressions

- **TRANSGENDER**: an umbrella term used to reference people whose gender identity differs from the sex they were assigned at birth, as well as to those individuals whose gender presentation differs from societal expectations regardless of use or hormones or surgery to physically transition.

- **TRANSSEXUAL:** refers to individuals whose gender identity differs from the sex that they were assigned at birth. Although similar to transgender, transsexual usually refers to individuals who physically/surgically/hormonally transition from one binary gender identity to another.

- **TRANS OR TRANS***: Similar to transgender, trans or transis an umbrella term used to describe individuals who identify outside of the gender binary, individuals whose gender identity differs from the sex they were assigned at birth, and individuals who defy transitional gender norms. Seen by some as a more inclusive umbrella term

- **GENDERQUEER:** a gender identity based in rejecting the gender binary, and instead understand gender as a spectrum. Folks who are genderqueer may see themselves as somewhere in between or may feel outside of that entirely. Many genderqueer feel constrained by societal binary gender and may use gender expression to subvert gender expressions and norms as political/social/personal statement.

- **CISGENDER:** Cis comes from the Latin root "cis" means to be on the same side. Cisgender is a term to refer to individuals who are not transgender, and feel as though their gender identity corresponds to the gender they were assigned at birth.

- **TRANNY:** a derogatory term slur that has historically been used to degrade trans people. Some trans people have reclaimed this term.

- **INTERSEX:** refers to an individual whose sex characteristics are ambiguous. Infants who are born with ambiguous external genitals are often subjected to increasingly controversial invasive surgeries to make their genitalia conform to their assigned gender. Often inappropriately conflated with transgender identity/experience.

- **HERMAPHRODITE**: a derogatory term formerly used to describe individuals who are intersex.

- **DRAG KING**: refers to a female assigned individual who dresses as male in an exaggerated gender focused theatrical performance.

- **DRAG QUEEN**: refers to a male assigned individual who dresses as female in an exaggerated gender focused theatrical performance.

- **FTM/F2M**: an acronym referring to someone who was assigned female at birth and now identifies as male

- **MTF/M2F**: an acronym referring to someone who was assigned male at birth and now identifies as female

- **TRANSGENDER WOMAN OR GIRL**: assigned male at birth a transgender woman or girl now identifies and/or lives presenting as female. May also just identify as a woman and see being transgender as part of a past medical history

- **TRANSGENDER MAN OR BOY**: assigned female at birth a transgender man or boy now identifies and/or lives presenting as male. May also just identify as a man and see being transgender as part of a past medical history.

- **ASSIGNED SEX**: the classification of an infant as either "male" or "female" based on improvise perceptions of presenting physical anatomy.

- **GENDER IDENTITY**: Everyone has a gender identity, it refers to ones internal sense of being female, male, or neither. For many trans people the gender they were assigned at birth does not match their gender identity.

♦ **GENDER PRESENTATION**: The way that you express your gender to the world via clothing, hair style/length, makeup, jewelry, or other gender coded adornment. Gender presentation doesn't always correspond to ones gender identity.

♦ **PGP**: Preferred Gender Pronoun.

♦ **GENDER BINARY**: a rigid system of categorizing gender into either "male" or "female". This system is restrictive for those whose identity or expression of gender doesn't fit into one of the rigid categories.

♦ **LGBTQQITSA**: Lesbian, gay, bisexual, trans, queer, questioning, intersex, two spirit, asexual often shortened to LGBTQ

♦ **TRANSPHOBIA**: fear, or discomfort about trans people. Similar to homophobia it may manifest as slurs, violence, or other discrimination (sometimes sanctioned by government)

A final note on terminology. Sometimes writers unfamiliar with trans community are tempted to utilize the word "real" to denote a person who isn't trans. Always avoid saying that a character you are writing is a "real boy" or a "real girl." To do so indicates that some people (trans people) aren't. All people are "real."

Pronouns

When writing trans and gender nonconforming characters pronouns are a tremendous part of getting the story right. While "he's" and "she's" might seem minor and unimportant part of your work as a writer, when writing about trans characters they take on a whole new level of importance.

Pronouns are the words that are used in language to denote the gender of a character. When characters are gender nonconforming pronouns can become more important and more complicated. When in the world trans people often experience being mispronounced either by accident—people not realizing (and asking) what pronoun a person would prefer, or maliciously as an act of gender-based violence. As such when writing stories with trans characters these three letter words carry a lot of weight. First rule about pronouns, don't misgender your characters unless it's part of a transphobic portion of your plot that your character is experiencing.

Some genderqueer or trans people use non-binary pronouns, these pronouns take the place of the female/male-gendered pronouns: she/her, he/his. There are numerous versions of non-binary pronouns. Two common examples of non-binary pronouns are: They/Their and Ze/Hir. In recent years use of the pronoun they has become increasingly popular amongst genderqueer communities, although there are numerous examples of non-binary pronouns.

> **They/Their: Sam had to go back to school because they left their backpack in their locker.**
>
> **Ze/Hir: Sam had to go back to school because ze left hir backpack in hir locker.**

As a genderqueer author I frequently use non-binary pronouns for characters in my books and stories. For me it's important personally and also politically as an activist. I want to write characters that reflect the community that I come from. If you are going to utilize non-binary pronouns in your writing, be prepared to defend your choice to publishers. Some editors will question the choice on grounds that they are improper English, for example the use of "they" as a singular pronoun vs. plural pronoun. In other instances editors/ publishers will raise concerns that readers may be confused by pronouns that they are unfamiliar with.

If you're going to use non-binary pronouns in your writing make sure that you used them correctly. Nothing says imposter faster than an incorrect use of pronouns in a story about a gender variant character. Also, be thoughtful about your choice of pronouns. Just a character needs to be well developed, and you wouldn't just randomly make them have a trans identity just for the sake of diversity in your book, non-binary pronouns should be approached with the same level of thoughtfulness and as part of deeper character development work. If one of my characters uses non-binary pronouns that's a decision that I feel very strongly about and one that I will defend to an editor/publisher to the point of being willing to pull my story from publication if they are unwilling to respect the pronouns of a character.

Now you are equipped with the basics of language not to necessarily go out and use it, but to at the very least move forward with your research and exploration about if you are wanting to include trans characters in your work, and how to talk about those characters, their experiences and identities.

Identity

There is no one right or wrong way to be trans, no prescriptive path around transition (or not) that trans people undergo. As I discussed in the terminology section above, there are as many ways to understand one's gender, as there are people in the world. The trans community is incredibly diverse but because of the limited representation in media, and YA literature in particular, it means that any book that makes its way onto a bookstore's shelves, is automatically going to hold a significant amount of cultural weight. It's a book that youth who are searching for support will find, that teachers/parents/librarians and other adults will read.

The trans identity of your characters should be as developed and nuanced as any other identity that character holds, or any other aspect of their life. It's not enough to just have a trans character in your book for the sake of having a trans character. To do so, is to create a one-dimensional character that won't be engaging or believable to your readers, especially any whom might be trans themselves. In order to create a believable trans character, in part you will as an author need to understand what being trans means to that character. Understanding that will give you the tools you need to write engaging and quality stories that are fully developed.

When writing about any character trans or otherwise one of the first character development questions I puzzle through is how my character understands their gender. Everyone has a gender identity and a gender expression, not just those whose experience and/or identity places them somewhere on the trans spectrum. I ask right alongside questions about age, race, religion/beliefs, geographic region, class, ability, body type, body modifications, education etc. These are the kind of basic initial details I need to know about my character regardless of how I think they will or won't fit into the larger storyline.

Specifically, when I am writing a character who is somewhere on the trans spectrum, how they define their gender is a first invaluable question that gives me a jumping off place to further examine who my character is, and how their gender variance will (or won't) factor into the storyline. I see this character development period as an essential opportunity to get into the mind of my character, to get to know them so that as I move forward with the writing process I am able to know how my character will respond to various scenes and scenarios that appear within the story.

Initial questions I need to answer if I'm going to write about my character's trans identity:

How does my character identify?

How does my character express their gender identity?

Is my character able to express their identity in all areas of their life?

If not, where can't they?

How does that make them feel?

How do other characters in the book respond to my character's gender identity and/or expression?

One of the basic mistakes that cisgender writers often make when initially trying to write about trans characters is to make the entire storyline revolve around the character's gender, or in most instances that character's gender change. Sometimes it's been done well, more often it's been done astonishingly badly but the important detail here is that it's been done. If you're wanting to write a YA novel featuring a trans character find a way to incorporate them into your work without making the entire book about their coming out, or transition to another gender

Trans identity might be a defining characteristic of your character, or it might not be. This is where the character development work becomes incredibly important so that you have a solid and holistic understanding of your character, giving you the information you need to have a solid understanding of how gender does and doesn't influence their life.

For some trans people they identify as being of a trans experience, but simply identify as male or female, and don't see having transitioned as being a defining aspect of their life. For these individuals, having been born a different gender than how they currently identify is part of their past, but not part of an identity that they have. How do you think it would be to write a character that is of trans experience but doesn't identify as trans? What if for them it's simply a reality of their body like having brown eyes, and brown hair but not an identity that they hold? How would that influence the way that you would create that character? How would you respectfully write about their gender without turning it into a focal point?

For other trans people (myself included) being trans is an important aspect of their life. Is your character an activist? Do they organize other youth around inequality? Have they had to fight for the right to live openly in their chosen gender expression? If so, their identity might be more of an interracial part of how they understand themselves, and so it might make sense that their trans identity would be more front and center within your story.

There is no one trans experience and thus no one universal way to write about trans characters. As an author your role is to understand your characters, to know who they are and part of that is how they understand their gender identity. But don't stop there, create nuanced characters, explore all the inersectonalities of who they are, how they identify and what their life experiences have been that have brought them to place and time where your book is set.

Bodies

There is an obsession within cisgender mainstream culture around what trans bodies look like, what trans people have done to their bodies to modify them etc. "Have you had the surgery" is a question that trans people encounter constantly. In reality, there is no one surgery that trans people have, but more importantly, the state of someone's genitals shouldn't be a topic of conversation.

When cisgender writers initially begin writing trans characters, often there is a tendency to get hung-up on the mechanics of physical transition. It's why so many stories with trans protagonists become coming out or transition-focused stories. In reality, each trans person will make individualized choices about what forms of physical transition related medical interventions they are or aren't interested in. There is not one-sized fits all approach to transition. The reality is that each trans person makes personal decisions at different times in their lives about what forms of transition related medical intervention they do or don't want. This may look like hormones only, having one surgery, having many surgeries, not taking hormones but having surgery(ies), or not having surgeries at all. The decision whether to access transition related medical care is extremely personal and based on a variety of complicated variables ranging from personal choice, to financial means. Transition related medical procedure are seen as "elective" and as such are generally not covered by medical insurance, thus creating incredible financial barriers for many trans people, and youth in particular.

The decision to physically alter one's body is extremely personal, and differs from trans person to trans person. Important to note is that although it has become a dominant narrative within the media, not all trans people hate their bodies. Similarly, not all trans people relate to a "trapped in the wrong body" narrative that the mainstream media has legitimated as the way to be trans (though of course there are trans people for whom that is their experience).

As you begin writing trans characters, as you would any character, particularly within the YA genre where puberty may be a relevant theme. Think about how your character understands their body at the time of the story. This doesn't need to necessarily make it into the book itself as a plot point—see above the overdone nature of the coming out narrative. However, this kind of information about your character will aid you as a writer in creating holistic character, and may inform the way you subtly talk about your character, and how they interact with the world around them. As you think about the ways in which your character understands their body at the time of the story, remember that an internal sense of gender is something that often shifts over time for all of us, not just those individuals on the trans spectrum. Just as you likely don't feel the same way about your gender and body as you did say as a high school freshman as you do today, your character understands their gender at the time of your story is likely different than they understood it five years ago, and both of those gender identities are possibly different from how your character will understand their gender five years in the future.

In most jurisdictions trans youth who are under the age of 18 need parental consent to legally access transition related medical care. A result is that most (though not all) trans teens do not have access to hormone blockers (to interrupt the effects of puberty), hormone replacement therapy, or surgery(ies) though they may choose to modify their bodies in different ways such as binding and tucking. In other instances, other trans youth may access hormones illegally.

Stereotypes

Because trans people are stigmatized and misunderstood within mainstream society there are a number of stereotypes about who trans people are. If you saw a trans person on *Law & Order* or a similar crime show, chances are you don't want to include anything resembling that storyline in your work. Your job as an author creating story lines about trans characters is to ensure that the stories you write don't play into those harmful stereotypes.

Stereotypes of trans people take many forms. There are stereotypes about trans people's bodies. Frequently trans people are represented as sex workers, or represented as being deceitful. Trans people are often portrayed as leading double lives and trick unsuspecting individuals into getting close only to surprise them, think the awful representation of trans women in *The Crying Game* where when a woman is revealed to be of trans experience, she's met with a man puking. All through the media, trans people are also vilified; frequently they are portrayed as sex workers.

Another increasingly common stereotype of trans people and specifically trans women are transitioning in order to gain access to women only spaces, namely public bathrooms, with the intent of attacking cisgender women. This should sound absurd to you, and yet it's an argument that has been used to mobilize public opinion in order to legalize gender based discrimination against trans people. Recently this issue came to the forefront in California where conservative politicians objected to a recently passed law that prohibits discrimination in schools and protects LGBTQ youth, including allowing trans youth to access sex-segregated school program programs and activities.

Bias crimes occur disproportionally to transgender people, especially transgender women of color. The 2012 National Coalition of Anti-Violence Programs reported that 73% of all anti-LGBTQ homicide victims in 2012 were people of color, and that 53% of all the anti-LGBTQ homicide victims in 2012 were transgender women. Trans people live with a daily fear of violence. As such, it makes sense that violence is portrayed in the stories we write but when it's done, it needs to be done with care and intention. Don't hurt the trans person in your story for the sake of hurting them, or worse without thought to what that violence represents. Be intentional, respectful and thoughtful if your trans character is going to be victim/survivor of violence.

I'm sure it goes without saying that your intention isn't to be transphobic in your writing. To do that requires research both to ensure that you're creating vibrant and well rounded characters, but also to ensure that you're avoiding transphobic pitfalls. Make your character as interesting as you would make any other character, never rely on a character's trans identity to be what makes them interesting, and if a character you're working on wasn't interesting don't make them trans in order to make them more engaging or compelling.

Reality

Unless your story featuring trans characters is set on another planet or some other alternate/fantasy reality, there are social/cultural realities that are important to at least be aware of as you are writing trans characters. Even if you aren't going to explicitly address these themes within the text of your work, being aware and conscious of the ways in which if not explicitly address within the text.

LGBT youth and trans and other gender nonconforming youth in particular experience high rates of bullying and harassment in school. The Gay, Lesbian and Straight Education Network (GLSEN)'s 2011 National School Climate Survey indicates that more than 8 out of 10 LGBT students experience some sort of harassment in school either from other students or teachers and administrators or both. LGBTQ youth are bullied 2-3 times more often than their straight counterparts, and trans and gender nonconforming youth. Particularly concerning is that only ten states in the United States have legislation that protects students from anti-LGBTQ harassment and bullying.

LGBTQ youth homelessness has reached epidemic proportions within the United States. Even though LGBTQ youth only make up 5-10% of youth in the United States 40% of all homeless youth identify as LGBTQ, and trans and other gender nonconforming youth are overrepresented within that statistic. LGBTQ youth experience exceptionally high rates of family rejection as a direct result of their sexual orientation and/or gender identity, The Center For American Progress indicates that 62% of LGBT youth report family rejection compared to 30% of their heterosexual homeless peers. According to the Center For American Progress, the average age that transgender youth become homeless is 14.4 years old; 58% of homeless gay or trans youth have been sexually assaulted.

Family rejection, bullying and discrimination in schools as well as hate crime violence like described earlier in the Chapter is a reality for trans people. While you don't necessarily have to explicitly write about transphobia in your stories, it is important to have these realities in mind as you research, work through character development and begin writing. I believe this is especially true if you hope to reach young trans readers with your stories.

Write diverse stories that youth deserve

Although there is an increased representation of trans characters within LGBT independent and small press published literature, including YA there unfortunately remains minimal and stereotypical representation within mainstream publishing. I believe that our job as YA authors is to write compelling stories that reflect the complicated worlds that youth of today are growing up in. Youth deserve honest stories that reflect their lives, identities and communities and part of that means ensuring that trans and gender variant youth are represented within our work

My hope is that this chapter has given you the information you need in order to think about more critically about the gender of the characters you are writing and helped you think about what it would mean to incorporate gender variant characters in your stories/books. This chapter isn't meant to tell you how to write trans characters, but rather my hope is that you are left with questions to investigate to guide you in developing complex characters of trans experience and otherwise. Youth deserve complicated diverse stories and that includes gender diversity. Even if you decide not to write trans characters, all of your future characters will benefit as part of your preliminary character development you examining what gender identity and expression means to them. Remember, everyone has a gender identity!

CHAPTER 9

Agent Secrets For YA Writers

Laurie McLean, Partner, Fuse Literary

Divine Secrets of the YA-YA Hood: Where Did YA Come From?

Young adult literature is, like teenagers themselves, a relatively new phenomenon. Before the previous Great Depression, the one in the 1930s, teenagers as we understand them did not exist. Children went to school until they dropped out to work in the fields or industry. Receiving a high school diploma was rare and the equivalent to receiving a college degree today.

Then came the economic crash of 1929. Because there were barely any jobs for adults, children were encouraged to stay in school as long as possible to hold young people out of the labor market for a few more years and thereby reduce competition. All of a sudden there was a new kind of American, the teenager, and they were searching for their place in society. And wondering who they were as people.

For decades teenagers read the same books as their parents, especially science fiction and fantasy (still a YA staple today). And libraries and bookstores included the few teen books they offered on one or two bookshelves in the children's section. This remained the case until paperbacks came out in the 1970s and S.E. Hinton's *The Outsiders* captured the attention of teens everywhere. Shortly thereafter teen sections began to crop up in big libraries and bookstores across the country, and accessible series like *Sweet Valley High* or R.L. Stine's *Fear Street* demonstrated the economic potential of the YA market.

Which brings us to the turn of the current century when YA fiction exploded in growth with the super-success of a boy wizard named Harry Potter. Not enough can be stated about J.K. Rowling's knack for getting teens to read as well as play videogames or sports. Reading was in jeopardy for this age group, but not anymore. This heroic effort was soon followed by the successes of Stephenie Meyer's *Twilight Saga* and Suzanne Collins's *Hunger Games* trilogy, making YA fiction today one of the most lucrative sections in the publishing industry.

As a literary agent, and primarily interested in the business component of the literary world, we try to surf the waves of popularity for future bestsellers. Therefore it came as no surprise that a tsunami of agent interest followed the huge success of YA literature in the early 2000s. YA fiction was the most experimental area of publishing in content, style, and tone. And when you add the power of the social media and online marketing tools that were ushered in during the past decade, it is easy to see why YA writing has become interesting even to longtime adult authors. Certainly it is appealing to newer writers who grew up reading wonderful teen tales and wanted to keep writing about that magical and special time in a person's life.

Agents of Chaos: What do Agents Do Exactly?

At the most basic level, a literary agent is an author's business partner. An agent locates a publisher interested in buying an author's writing and then negotiates a deal. But a literary agent is so much more than that. An agent is:

- A scout who constantly researches what publishers are looking for
- An advocate for an author and his or her work
- A midwife who assists with the birth of a writing project
- A reminder who keeps the author on track if things begin to slip
- An editor for that last push before submission
- A critic who will tell authors what they need to hear in order to improve
- A matchmaker who knows the exact editors for an author's type of writing
- A negotiator who will fight to get the best deal for an author
- A mediator who can step in between author and publisher to fix problems

- A reality check if an author gets out of sync with the real world
- A liaison between the publishing community and the author
- A cheerleader for an author's work or style
- A focal point for subsidiary, foreign and dramatic rights
- A mentor who will assist in developing an author's career
- A rainmaker who can get additional writing work for an author
- A career coach for all aspects of your writing future
- An educator about changes in the publishing industry
- A manager of the business side of your writing life

An author should interview an agent as they would a publicist, printer or any other business partner and not be star struck to the point of accepting the first agent who offers representation. I believe an author should find an agent with the following characteristics:

- Integrity
- Wisdom
- Knowledge (different from wisdom)
- A strong work ethic
- A personality fit (this becomes even more important as your career develops)
- A personal commitment to their profession (they should be developing their careers too!)

- A professional relationship with you (not just a friend, but a partner)

It helps when you enter a relationship to know what you want to get out of it—and to be able to articulate this to your agent business partner. Do you want someone who will hold your hand, or a shark who will get you the last dime possible from a book contract? They're not usually the same person. Do you want an editing agent to help you polish your work prior to submitting to editors? Or do you want a strict business-oriented agent who will concentrate solely on pitching your work and negotiating deals on your behalf? Do you want someone who's fun to work with or do you prefer a no-nonsense, results-oriented personality?

Once you build a profile for what you want in an agent, you improve the probability that the agent who becomes your partner will work out well long-term.

Basically an agent collects 15% of any deal they negotiate for a client as the total payment for their services. For foreign deals or movie/television/stage deals they may charge 20%, which is split with a co-agent who specializes in these subsidiary rights. Some ask for reimbursement for nominal out-of-pocket expenses, but those are minimal since we've moved into the era of email and internet. But do check an agency's expense reimbursement policy before you sign a contract. If you don't like what you see, ask the agent about it. Put an addendum in the contract limiting out-of-pocket expenses incurred on your behalf without your approval. And if you can't live with what the agency charges for expenses, don't sign the contract. There are hundreds of agents out there. Keep looking.

Do Your Homework! Finding the Right Agent for You

I hope that subhead did not cause flashbacks to your high school days when projects were overdue or tests were looming. By doing your homework I was referring to researching who you want to work with in an agent and/or publishing house.

At conferences I often urge aspiring authors to spend 10 percent of the time it took them to write their novel or nonfiction book and apply that towards finding their publishing business partners. All literary agencies are now online. Nearly all of them have websites that tell you about the history of the company, the personnel, the deals they've made and how to submit your work. Many agents have their own blogs as well, where they share their personal thoughts about publishing and information about the industry. And even more agents are on Twitter and/or Facebook, as well as Tumblr, Pinterest, Google+ and other social media platforms.

By following or friending them you will get great insight into their personalities as well as what they are up to on a daily basis.

Editors too are on social media in a big way. You can see what books they're excited about, what they have just acquired, trends in the YA market, and what they do not wish to see. Not as many editors have blogs, but when they do you can almost guarantee yourself a crash course in excellent writing.

I advise writers to begin with one of the helpful agent search engines, such as agentquery.com, querytracker.net, pubmatch. org and others. By clicking on the box of what you write (in this case "Young Adult Fiction"), you will be presented with a list of a hundred or so literary agents who have described themselves as representing YA fiction. But don't stop there.

The next step is to visit the websites of each of these agents. Follow them on social media. Google them and read interviews with them. Now you can begin to prioritize your list into A, B, and C tiers. 'A' would contain your top wish list agents, 'B', the next desirable, and so on.

You will also learn exactly how each agent likes to receive queries and what components they should contain. You'll discover the typical timeframe for their decision. You should create a spreadsheet or database so you'll know when to follow up with each agent. I know you're thinking, "Wow, why can't the agents all accept how *I* want to submit my work to them," but there really is method to our seeming madness.

I personally receive between 1,000-1,500 queries per month. I have an assistant go through each one and she either rejects them or passes them along to me to see if I want to read more pages. We have to take an assembly-line approach where the queries are all similar in format to make the writing jump out. Otherwise we would end up judging the query instead of the writing.

I apologize to you right now for that extra work. But remember that 10% of your writing time dedicated to querying? This is part of it. The more you personalize your pitch to each agent, the better your chances of winning representation.

Another piece of advice is not to send your query out to all the agents you've identified in one big burst. That might seem like a time-saver, but you are really shooting yourself in the foot.

If you send your query to the A list first, and one or more agents replies with a revise and resubmit letter, you can fix the problems they've identified with your submission and resubmit it to them. You can then send your revised submission to the B list. If you've already queried all the agents who handle what you write, and you learn about a way to make your manuscript better, you cannot submit a revision if they are considering an earlier version. It comes across as desperate and a pain in the neck for the agent to find your original query and amend it. We simply don't have the time so we don't do it. Sorry, but that's the truth.

To better the chances that your query will grab an agent's attention, make it brief, make it personal (say you like a client's work or congratulate them on a recent deal), make it interesting (more like a movie trailer than a dry accounting of the story), eliminate all grammatical errors (ask a friend to read it since it is common knowledge that a writer cannot find his or her own typos), and infuse it with your voice if you can. A referral from one of the agent's clients will propel you to the top of the heap. But don't try to solicit a referral from an author you don't know or just met. They rarely comply.

Don't Sink your Sub!

In the old days, prior to the wonders of self-publishing, writers would put early manuscripts in a desk drawer, pulling them out years later and marveling at what they thought were bestselling books…diamonds in the rough that turned out to be badly cut glass. Today, the number one problem I see over and over again in my digital stack of queries is submitting your work before its time.

Don't get me wrong. I love self-publishing. I truly believe it gives writers opportunities that they never before had access to. But just because you can publish a book doesn't mean you should. And I'm not talking about manuscripts filled with typos and grammatical errors. I'm talking about books that would have benefited from another thoughtful editing pass, or another round of critiques from your professional network of publishing pals (not your family or class at school), or a run through crowdsourced sites like Scribd or Wattpad.

I read submissions that have oodles of potential but just don't deliver on it. The writing is clunky or the dialogue stilted or the pacing uneven. I read a lot of submissions that tell me the writer hasn't quite reached that point in his or her professional development yet where the creative ideas match nicely with the level of their writing craft.

My colleague calls this "premature publication". I call it a live-and-learn lesson.

Sure, you can submit that first novel you worked so hard on. But when you query 25 agents and get 25 form rejections, don't automatically assume these agents don't know what they're talking about. Perhaps it's time to put that manuscript in a folder on your computer and start working on the next one. You'll have learned so much from that first writing experience, it's almost certain that the next one will be even better.

Publishing is a VERY Small Industry

And speaking about rejections, do whatever you have to do to deal with the sadness, frustration, and anger of having your work passed on by an agent or editor. But do it in the privacy of your own personal space. Never let it boil over into the public domain. And by this I mean Twitter and Facebook as well as an email to the rejectors calling them stupid or mean or unqualified.

I've received emails calling me names and threatening me. I have a special file folder for these emails in case something horrible happens.

I have also received emails from writers I've rejected who don't threaten me, but do say things like, "If you'd only gotten to Chapter three, that's when the story really takes off. But since you only asked for the first 10 pages you'll never know that you rejected the next J.K. Rowling!"

It is to your advantage to make that first sentence, first paragraph, first scene, and first Chapter, so excellent that the agent will have no choice but to ask to read more. Do a search on "best first lines in books" for inspiration and really dig deep. Is your first line unforgettable? Here are some examples of great first lines:

♦ "As Gregor Samsa awoke one morning from uneasy dreams he found himself transformed in his bed into a monstrous vermin." Franz Kafka, *Metamorphosis* (1915)

♦ "It was a bright, cold day in April, and the clocks were striking thirteen." George Orwell, *1984* (1949)

♦ "When Mr. Bilbo Baggins of Bag End announced that he would shortly be celebrating his eleventyfirst birthday with a party of special magnificence, there was much talk and excitement in Hobbiton" J.R.R. Tolkien, *The Fellowship of the Ring* (1954)

♦ "It's a funny thing about mothers and fathers. Even when their own child is the most disgusting little blister you could ever imagine, they still think that he or she is wonderful." Roald Dahl, *Matilda* (1988)

♦ "Mr. and Mrs. Dursley of number four Privet Drive were proud to say that they were perfectly normal, thank you very much." J.K. Rowling, *Harry Potter and the Philosopher's Stone* (1997)

You Want to Have a Career in Publishing? Act Professionally!

Writing is a very solitary, creative endeavor. It can be done, and often is, while wearing sweats or pajamas or casual clothing in the privacy of your own home at all hours of the day or night. But when the individual, private, creative endeavor of writing eventually meets the public business of publishing, sparks fly.

Agents are often the first brick wall writers run into when they take the work they've labored so hard to create into the light of day and discover it's not marketable or too long or too short or not written to sell. So, like rejections, it is very much in your best interest to learn from these lessons and apply them to future writing.

If you are going to meet an agent or editor at a workshop or conference or other event, think about how you want to present yourself. I'm not saying you have to wear a ballgown or suit. But look like you are worth the money you want to earn from your writing.

At conferences, dress is usually described as "business casual." That means a nice pair of pants, button-down shirt or polo shirt and shoes for the men, and dresses or pantsuits or skirts and blouses for the women.

If you decide you want to stand out by wearing a kilt (I've seen it) or kimono (I've heard about it) or goth-punk attire, be fully aware of the impression you're making. Ask yourself if you want to be known for your writing or your personal image.

I Can't Hear You! Why Voice is Essential in YA

So let's get down to the nitty-gritty. What do agents look for in YA writing?

The six rules of writing, it's been said, are:

Read. Read. Read.

Write. Write. Write.

And this goes for the YA market just as it does for anything else in writing. You need to develop an authentic teen voice if you're going to write about teen characters…and teen protagonists are the lifeblood of YA literature.

My number one answer to the oft-asked question, "What do you look for in YA writing?" is voice. It's also the most difficult to define.

When I say voice, I mean the author's ability to create a distinctive tone and message for their characters, which results in a unique, memorable story. Voice is that amazing, powerful part of a writer's skillset that infuses everything you create. It's your personality, sure. But it's also a combination of character development, dialogue, sentence structure, style, tone, and technique in your writing that makes it solely your own.

It's the difference between singing an original song you wrote and following along word-by-word on a Karaoke machine.

You develop your unique voice by writing. A lot. I tell my clients to write every day. Give yourself a goal and stick to it. It lubricates your writer mind and becomes easier as you go along. My client Julie Kagawa sets a goal of 1,000 words a day. If she reaches that goal early, she can go do other fun things. If it takes her all day and half the night, so be it. That's how she can turn out such wonderful stories at a rate of 2-3 per year.

But say you're not a teenager anymore and you still want to

write about that time in a person's life. That's where the "Read. Read. Read." advice comes in. You need to read all the YA books you can get your hands on. And not just in the genre you plan to write in. Read contemporary school drama YA to get a feel for how teens interact during the day. Read issues-oriented YA to see what serious problems these teens and their friends are facing. Read YA fantasy to become familiar with a genre that teens have loved all their lives. Even read YA nonfiction for research and information.

Another way to achieve a realistic teen voice in your dialogue is to hang out with teens and listen to the rhythm, tone and words they use. I am not advocating that you copy their speech patterns 100% in your writing. Especially since each new generation of teens seems to bring their own unique flare to their conversations. For fiction especially, your dialogue should be an exaggeration or approximation of conversations, not a verbatim replication. If you hang out at the food court at your local mall on a Saturday afternoon, you'll get the gist of what teens are interested in, as well as how they talk to one another and how they interact in a group. You'll eventually discover the tropes of their generation and their class structure or pecking order. It will help you decide if your dialogue is out of date or too weird. And you may find slang you can use as flourishes to keep your writing fresh.

Next up are the characters. They have to be interesting and unique enough for the reader to want to accompany them on the journey of the story. And they must hook the reader's attention in the first scene of the book. The protagonist must be flawed, not perfect. They must have room for growth and character development. They need to be fragile enough that the reader (and agent) roots for them to succeed even if they've got a chip the size of Australia on their shoulder. We need to love them despite their flaws and create an emotional connection with them.

As the author, you need to know your characters inside and out to be able to make them unique, memorable and consistent to their personal codes. Most of my clients make story "bibles" with character boards that not only list the characters' physical and emotional traits, but they also find photos of people who look like their characters (at least in their minds) complete with hair and eye color, physique, hobbies, etc. If your characters don't feel real to you, they will never feel real to your reader.

You also must have such a high level of dramatic intensity that it tortures your characters. Amp up their internal and external conflicts, then increase them even higher. Drive the pacing. You think the stakes are high? Make them higher. Readers must be squirming in their seats throughout the story right alongside your characters. And climaxes are your opportunity to make your readers cry. Do it!

If I love the voice of the manuscript, its characters, and its intensity, then I also look at a writer's proficiency with grammar, spelling and other basic writing skills. I examine world building, which is important even if the story takes place in our real modern world. The elements described in the world must feel real and alive to the readers. Oftentimes setting can be as important as character in a book.

Besides all these factors, you also need to know the basics of what publishers are looking for. YA manuscripts are mainly between 60,000-80,000 words long, although some can be longer if the story warrants it. (Don't just overwrite and use this as an excuse to pitch a 250,000 word YA fantasy. It will earn you a check mark rejection.) At an average of 250 words per page, that translates into 240 to 320 pages. You can't really use Microsoft Word's word count feature to accurately reflect word count, since there are approximately 350-400 words on a text-heavy MS Word page. However, for purposes of telling an agent or editor your word count, you can feel free to put MS Word count = XXX on the top of your submission or query letter.

I doubt I need to say this, but I will anyway. YA novels feature protagonists in high school...12-18 years old. If you've got an older protagonist, you might have written a new adult novel or an adult book. And if they're younger, you've written a middle-grade or Chapter book. Know your market.

Finally, I'd like to say something about trends. Don't follow them. In YA literature especially, you cannot write fast enough to keep up with trends. The only way you could capture a trend and capitalize on it is if you'd already written a book when the trend swings your way.

My advice is to write the book you're passionate about. Think back to why you are writing a YA book in the first place and create the book of your heart. If you love what you're writing, so will readers. So will agents. So will editors.

I hope this has given you some idea of what an agent looks for in a YA submission. Now go out and create a story that is unique, not derivative, with characters who leap off the page and cause readers to laugh, cry and want to read your book all over again once they've finished!

CHAPTER 10

Book Bloggers Are
Your Friends

Pam van Hylckama Vlieg, Bookalicious.org

With our nation's newspapers tightening budgets and slashing the literature section, book bloggers have stepped up to fill that role. Bloggers, however, write quite differently than newspaper reviewers do, and in some cases bloggers are more popular and have better Search Engine Optimization (SEO) than the authors they are reviewing. This is the Wild Wild West of internet-land and this chapter will teach you everything you need to know about book bloggers.

I've seen bloggers do amazing things. I've seen them make a self-published book rise on the Amazon charts. I've also watched as one of our collective favorite authors got her print run cut in half, so bloggers started an awareness program that lead to her getting reviews in trade magazines and a second printing before the book launched!

Bloggers can help you reach your target audience and are well versed in reaching readers in the genres in which they specialize. A profound love of books propels a blogger into working a full-time blogging job after working full-time day job hours.

We love authors, we love books, and we love book blogging!

Defining Book Bloggers

Book bloggers are like a giant tsunami washing over the publishing world. For good or bad we are here to stay, and I believe collectively can make an impact on the industry, title by title. There are bloggers for certain genres. Bloggers solely for audiobooks. Some only catalogue what they personally read and don't accept any review requests. One thing they will all have in common is a love of books.

When I started Bookalicious five years ago there were only a few bloggers around. Now there are thousands, and each of these unique people are putting a different spin on how to write a book blog.

In the most basic sense, a book blog is a blog about books.

How can they help you?

Bloggers can help an author in a myriad of ways. The most important way is reading your book and getting excited about it. A blogger that is behind a book one hundred percent will write a favorable review (in their own style, maybe even with pictures or GIFs) and then tout that review on all of their social networking sites. This, at times, creates a little wave that will keep growing as it heads to the shore causing a rise in sales. Then, hopefully, other bloggers will pick up and love the book as well.

Do not be discouraged if the blogger doesn't like your book. Thoughtful negative reviews can sell just as many copies as a love-fest, if not more! Once I remember saying on my blog that I hated a book because of its insta-love and needy boys. My comments exploded with readers who love that sort of thing and they promised to purchase the book. I once read a review where a blogger said they disliked boarding school drama. I love that kind of book, so I bought it.

Never engage with a blogger on a review. Even if they have a detail wrong about your book.

"I'm sorry to bother you, blogger, but that isn't a dung beetle shifter, it is a rove beetle shifter."

Just don't do it. There's no little black book of blacklisted authors but word does get around fast, especially if a blogger decides to blog about you.

Never refer to the copy you gave them as a "gift." We get plenty of free books and none of them are a gift. They are work for our blog. Five hours of reading, two hours of writing and formatting a post, and then another few minutes of social media.

We'll get into more do's and don'ts later. But the main way a blogger can help you is by accepting your book for review, reading it, and giving it a review whether it is flattering or not.

How To Find A Blogger Who Writes About Your Genre

Google is your friend. When I look for reviews of a certain book I search for the name of the book and the word "review" or "blog review." Then I click through what the search engine finds. You'll be able to tell the quality and influence of the blog by the comments, the design, and by clicking on the social media icons and checking out their stats.

Use search engines to find compatible titles to your works. Base your research on the bloggers who covered those books.

When you find the bloggers you want to work with, follow them on social media. A great way to find bloggers is to see who the blogs you like are talking to. They will most likely be talking to other awesome bloggers at different levels in the blogosphere that cover likeminded genres.

Also check the sidebars of the blogs you find. Some will have a handy list of bloggers they like to read.

Here are a few questions to ask yourself:

- Is the blog's design clean and easy to navigate?

- Does the blog get comments on most posts?

- Do the posts read at a high school level of language? (Below or above means less readers.)

- Does the blog have a review policy easy to find?

- Do you like the way the posts read?

It is exhausting to look at each blog individually, but it is necessary. Try to remember there is a person, or persons, behind each blog and being able to contact them with knowledge of their blog is very important. It could give you a serious leg up on your competition.

If you follow authors on Twitter and Facebook that write in your genre, pay attention to who they talk to. Then research the blogger the same way you would if you found them on your search.

While you are looking at the blogs and compiling a mental list of impressive ones, why not make a spreadsheet? If you find a blogger who doesn't do your genre you never know if you will write in that genre later and will need that info then.

Items on the spreadsheet could include:

- Name of the blog

- Email address found on the review policy

- URL
- Genres covered
- Social Media links
- Your personal 1-10 rating of the blog
- Name of the person running the blog

When you have researched and feel you have a good twenty or thirty blogs that you would like to pitch it is time to contact the blogger.

How To Query A Blogger

Contacting a blogger is a lot like contacting an agent. They are generally looking for a reason to say no, just like an agent. They receive just as many queries, and their requests come from publicists, PR companies, and authors. A lot of bloggers do not like dealing with the author directly at all. Make sure to read the review policy carefully.

Never approach a blogger about your book on social media, or in their blog comments. Always send a concise polite email. If you do choose to email never attach your book. Let the blogger answer your email with a yes and then move forward. Most bloggers have a no-response-means-no policy. Which means if they do not respond to your pitch within three weeks then they probably aren't going to and there's no need to follow up.

It is always best to send a paper copy of your book and an advance copy if possible. Paper becomes inherently more important in reviewing land. Probably because the books are sitting there staring the blogger in the face. Why haven't you read me yet? I need at least four months in advance but I run a big blog with over twenty contributors. Two months in advance is the absolute minimum in contacting bloggers for review. If you really need to wait for your finished copies, (I'd beg some more ARCs from my publisher) then send the email out a month in advance and let them know you are waiting for those. If you're self-publishing make sure to ask the blogger which review format they like: Kindle, EPUB, or PDF.

You may not get many responses. And that's okay. As I mentioned earlier there are thousands of blogs in the world. You should arrange the blogs you've found and put in your spreadsheet in waves. Email your top must-haves first, then go down the list until you have the amount of blogs you want reading your book. The bigger blogs are generally busier and even if they accept a book it doesn't mean they will for sure read and review it. My personal review policy states that acceptance of a book is not a promise of review.

For me the reasons are simple. Maybe it was a 'meh' book for me, or I just never got time to read it. Maybe I started reading it and just didn't like it and stopped. I only review books that I finished in their entirety and novels that elicit some sort of reaction from me. Meh doesn't help me with my hit count. No one cares about meh reviews.

Here's an example of a pitch I'm writing to my blog.

Dear Pam,

I've been reading Bookalicious for quite a while and I love that interview you did with <Author>. Because of that interview I thought you might like to see a copy of my book for possible review.

My book, NORTHANGER ABBEY AND NECROMANCERS is a take on Jane Austen's original work. It is set in the world of Austen's NORTHANGER ABBEY but follows a young necromancer who keeps accidentally pulling characters into this story from Austen's other works and ruining her canon. When Darcy falls in love with Emma and they have an affair the other characters of the book decide to fight back, find the necromancer, and put a stop to his villainy.

My publisher, Not Yo Mama's Books (or if you're self published, I...) would be glad to send you a copy in whatever format you prefer.

You can find out more about me and my novel at:

Goodreads: <link>

Twitter: <link>

Blog: <link>

Best,

<Author>

If you can, offer an incentive like a giveaway for their readers. Never offer to pay a blogger or buy them a gift card for their review. That is one of the highest insults in our land. But something for their readers is generally appreciated, and if they don't do contests they will decline the extra stuff.

With agents you follow up every three months or so to see if they have gotten to your submission. With bloggers I would follow up once on release day to say I hope you've decided to read it and that you enjoy it. Following up makes the blog and your book feel even more like work. No one wants their blog to feel like work and your book will move down and down in the review pile until it is gone completely if you make the blogger uncomfortable.

Which brings us to...

Blogger/Author Relationships

There are a few very important rules to remember. Bloggers are not your friends, or your peers, or free labor. They are your target audience. Albeit they are smarter about the industry side of reading than the average reader they are still your target audience.

You can most definitely be friendly with bloggers. I love talking on Twitter to my favorite authors and having drinks with them at conferences but I don't tell them my secrets. The line has to be drawn somewhere to still remain professional and have a critical eye. In the few cases that a true friendship has grown out of these drinks and Twitter fun, I have stopped reviewing the author due to conflict of interest.

A blogger isn't held to journalistic standards but our word is our currency. The bigger the blog the more careful you need to be with your ethical standards. One wrong move and the pack will take you down from alpha position and a new alpha will move in. It is a very Nat Geo world.

The same goes for authors. If you contact a blogger for more than the initial "will you read my book" email you set yourself up to be made example of. There is a lot of drama in the blogging/author world. It reminds me of the East Coast/West Coast rapper wars of the nineties. Conversation based on negative reviews is uncomfortable and bloggers will turn to their blogs to work out their feelings about being contacted about their review. Because we are not journalists and our blogs are very personal for us it is best just not to contact bloggers you aren't friendly with outside of the review request.

A few simple rules on relationships:

- Never respond to a negative review. Even to say thanks. Do not tweet it. If you need to vent, vent to your friends or via email to your author friends. Never grieve publicly.

- Don't follow a blogger on Twitter and start talking to them all the time after they get your book. We know it's fake and that you'll stop talking to us as soon as our review is up.

- Do talk to us as if you are super interested or think we are the bee's knees. Chances are we think you're cool too.

- Do not follow up on an unanswered review request or a book that is not being reviewed.

- For the love of the book gods, do not go to Goodreads and read your reviews. And if you do, please do not engage.

- Do not comment on reviews of your books. It stifles the comments for some reason.

- Do send an email if you wish to thank a blogger for a review if the review is mostly positive.

What Can You Expect From A Blogger?

That depends greatly on the blogger. As I said before each blog is different, but by looking closely at the blogs you want to target you can learn what to expect from each.

Most bloggers do not blog to help you promote books. It all comes back to that love of reading and books that I keep talking about. Remember that when wondering what to expect from a blogger. We aren't PR machines and free advertising.

For example, Bookalicious takes many different kinds of posts. Guest posts by authors, content provided by publishers, giveaways, and marketing posts (put this widget on 100 blogs and get a three Chapter excerpt!). So if you're smart with how you contact my blog you can have a day completely filled with your book! But you can never expect a review from my blog, because I don't promise a review. But I can promise to put your guest post and giveaway up on a certain day bringing a small amount of awareness to your title.

Some bloggers are highly organized with posting calendars and regulate what and when they can accept these types of marketing posts. Others, like myself, are more open and can throw things up with just a bit of notice.

Blogs are mostly run like a small business. It is a labor of love as most blogs make no money and what little advertising they do have is used to pay hosting costs.

It is also good to be clear about what bloggers can expect for you, the author, or your publishing company. Cross-marketing is good for everyone involved. If you write a guest post please be around to answer the comments on the blogger's website. If they write about you then make sure to put it out on your social media, or better yet, write a little blog post about where you have been featured for the week. The more you give the more it will come back to you and bloggers love to get in on a campaign that is going both ways marketing wise.

So You're Ready To Pitch A Blogger!

I know this may seem a bit overwhelming. So many etiquette rules and each blog is different. I know that researching blogs will be more time intensive than researching your book. But in the end I do think it is worth it to be thoughtful and personable when approaching bloggers.

If you have any questions about the material in this Chapter please use the bio below to contact me. I'll try to help, because I'm a blogger and like any blogger I love authors and books.

My Favorite Ya Book Blogs:

Chick Loves Lit
http://chickloveslit.com

Shanyn focuses on contemporary/realistic YA. She is one of those super organized bloggers I mentioned before, so make sure you reach out in advance if you want her to include your book in her lineup.

Good Books and Good Wine
http://goodbooksandgoodwine.com

April covers most genres and tends to lean toward the speculative, fantastical and strange. I love her approach to reviews and I do believe she schedules pretty loosely as well. I'd definitely contact her if your book is dark or quirky.

Cuddlebuggery
http://cuddlebuggery.com

These ladies put the sass in YA fiction. The reviews are brutally honest and if you can hack that without crying into your keyboard then this is a great blog to pitch a debut work to. They have a good reach of readers and a fun style.

Forever Young Adult
http://foreveryoungadult.com

I don't personally like their review style, it is a bit too pop culture-y for me, but I'm the only one. These ladies give honest reviews and have a massive audience. They are pioneers in the GIF review sect of blogging and seem like fun gals to know. Bonus points for drinking games.

The Midnight Garden
http://themidnightgarden.net

Wendy Darling writes very thoughtful and very critical reviews and she's one of the biggest reviewers that Goodreads has ever seen. She reviews YA across the board and I would assume she needs a large lead-in time for reviews and other types of post. I really love pretty much every post she writes.

YA Bibliophile
http://yabibliophile.com

Heidi is a school librarian and her love of kid-lit is coupled with her job. I love her blog because it comes from a librarian's perspective as well as a YA loving nerd standpoint. Heidi is a great reviewer who puts a thoughtful touch into everything she does.

I've done a quarter of your research for you! I almost forgot to tell you the most important rule of dealing with bloggers: Have fun! We're a fun bunch of book lovers who want to get the word out about your books.

CHAPTER 11

The Best About Collaboration (and a little of the worst)

Clay and Susan Griffith

You just had an incredible brainstorming session with a friend and hashed out the plot for a great new epic fantasy novel. But are you ready to write a book, or even a series together? Do you have what it takes to turn a night of literary passion into a long creative relationship of literary production?

Collaboration isn't for everyone. There's good, and there's bad. Some of it is thrilling and satisfying; some of it is brutal and angry.

Just like marriage.

...By the way, we're married.

Everybody's path to collaboration is different, but they all go through similar milestones. When we met, for instance, we were both writers trying to get published. We continued to write and to publish a few things separately. In 1995, Clay got a call from an editor he had worked for at Marvel Comics who asked him if he had any ideas for Disney comics. Clay confidently boasted he'd have half a dozen pitches on the editor's desk the next day. He hung up the phone and went straight to Susan because he knew little about Disney, but she knew everything. Before long our first co-written work was published—a comic book based on *Toy Story*.

That origin story of our collaboration highlights what we later found was the secret to our successful partnership. We each brought unique strengths to the work. Clay had already written comics and knew the format. He also wrote humor and material for children. Susan knew the subject and what makes Disney characters so popular.

We found that collaboration to be pretty painless, so we kept doing it. Before we knew it, we were no longer writing anything on our own. Everything was a joint venture. Over the next few years, we wrote more comics and short stories together, and then branched out with the successful *Vampire Empire* series from Pyr Books.

We were predisposed to collaborate even before the Disney comics. Even when we wrote solo, we had always read and edited each other's work. However, that is very different than a true collaboration. As a solitary writer you don't have to listen to suggestions from a reader. You don't have to fold their ideas and voice into your work if you think it changes your vision. With a collaborator, you do have to listen, and you do have to blend your voices. And that's the really tricky part.

A Few Words Before You Start Collaborating

Since we are married, there are elements to our collaboration that are a little different from a purely professional partnership. However, it isn't as different as you might suspect. And just as you wouldn't jump into a marriage without thinking about it (unless you're an impulsive lunatic), before you even start a collaborative writing project there are a few things to hash out to make the process run as smoothly as possible.

You may not want to worry about legal issues, but you'd better. You need a contract of some sort. We have a contract and it's called a marriage license. We already co-own everything in our lives whether it's the bank account, the house, the cat, or the copyright of a novel. The only way our property gets separated is if we get a divorce and we let our lawyers settle who owns what.

A good presentation of the types of things you need to think about before entering into a collaboration is laid out by writer Holly Lisle in a terrific essay (http://hollylisle.com/how-to-collaborate-and-how-not-to). It's not callous or selfish to plan ahead. It's smart, and it will save heartache and perhaps money later. It will force you to spell out a number of issues about the collaboration such as how do you divide the work? How do you divide the money? How do you decide what to work on as the partnership progresses? How do you divide the ownership and control of the properties you create?

Those issues are all important. They don't tend to be stumbling blocks for us. We pick our projects based on what excites both of us; if either says no, then it's no. All the money is ours equally, just like all the money we make from normal 8 to 5 jobs or the gold we take from stray leprechauns. Likewise, we co-own all our intellectual property and it isn't possible for either of us to exploit it without the cooperation or blessing of the other. And we will talk more about how we divide the actual writing work a little later.

There is, however, one pre-nuptial topic that you need to address in an agreement that is a big deal for us, and that is: Who has the last word? What if you get to a point in the book where you can't decide whether Steve dies at the end of the book? You have solid artistic reasons for killing Steve. Your partner has equally powerful arguments for letting Steve live. You two go back and forth on the topic day after day after day. After day. At some point, someone has to say "That's it. We're killing Steve (or we're not killing Steve)." Otherwise Steve is going to kill your book. The losing partner has to accept the decision and move on.

In our collaboration, we call this step the Nuclear Option. We have it in our unwritten agreement, but we have never used it. The partner who has the Button is whoever has the *lead* on any particular project. The Lead is the person who originated the job. It could be that the story was their original idea. It could be they found the editor or publisher the project is going to. Or they understand the market for the project best. The Lead can invoke the Nuclear Option to end a disagreement over content.

Why have we never used this awesome power? Because much like the nuclear option in the real world, once invoked, the world changes and you can never go back to pre-war times. Such exertion of authority defeats the point of collaboration. Our rule of thumb is that if one partner just won't shut up about Steve staying alive, the Steve-killer partner owes it to the validity of the process to take a harder look at the other person's argument. They might be right. Maybe you should trust them. Steve should live.

All that said, you must still have someone with access to the Button in case of a never-ending stalemate, or a simple inability to decide between two equally terrific paths. At some point, a final decision has to be made so production can continue. If the Nuclear Option is used frequently, however, you may be in a very unequal collaboration with a partner who prefers to be the winner of a scorched earth rather than an equal in a world that isn't totally his own. That's no fun, and not very satisfying artistically.

Now We're Ready To Collaborate. What Can We Expect?

PART A: We'll Start With the Bad Stuff

Now that we've outlined a few details you should iron out before going into the relationship, here are some of the challenges we have faced, and we suspect you and your partner will face, on the road to a finished project. Don't panic. They aren't fatal. Usually.

THERE WILL BE BLOOD. You will argue. Disagreements are almost inevitable. Oh sure, it's possible you will have the perfect dream collaboration where there are no problems or differences of opinion. Where the words flow like wine and you laugh the livelong day away and unicorns bring you new printer ink cartridges every time you run out. Congratulations. We hate you.

The bottom line is no two people—particularly two writers—can agree on everything all the time. So go ahead and argue, or discuss, or debate, or converse—whatever you call it. *Differences of opinions are valuable.* And they have to be settled either through compromise or by choosing one side over the other (see the dreaded Nuclear Option above) for the project to move forward. Here are some tips we discovered.

ARGUMENT LESSON #1: LISTEN TO THE OTHER PERSON. No really. Listen to them. When they say "I've got a problem with Steve in the last Chapter you wrote" do NOT hear "I hate the way you write and you've been trying to ruin this book from the beginning." Don't roll your eyes and go into *Fine, what's your petty quibble now?* mode. Because then both partners are suddenly defensive and aggressive, and nothing will get done except throwing up walls around personal turf. So don't do it. Listen. Even if it is yet another petty quibble about Steve. Listen.

ARGUMENT LESSON #2: BE CONSTRUCTIVE. Don't just say "I don't like this part." If you're going to make a criticism, the burden is on you to explain yourself. You have to be able to say why you don't like it. And, even better, you should make a suggestion on how to fix it. If you think Steve is too angry in Chapter 12 when Glamorgan the dragon destroys his castle, you have to be able to explain why Steve shouldn't be so angry. And how would you change Steve's disposition to make the Chapter better? In other words, don't just gripe. Be constructive. Offer alternatives. Bring something to the table to talk about. Then the odds are better it will be a conversation rather than an argument.

ARGUMENT LESSON #3: BE POSITIVE. Sometimes. Even assuming you've mastered the skill of offering reasons and viable alternatives when you criticize, you shouldn't criticize exclusively. You mother said if you can't say something nice, don't say anything at all. Well, she was wrong. But you can't just speak to your partner when you don't like something. Tell them when something is good too. Fight scene was thrilling? Say so. Character bit was perfectly layered into action? Tell them. Sex scene was smoking hot? Mention it. Compliments will not only soften the many coming hammer blows of "This part doesn't work," but it also creates discussion about what is good about the work, not just what's bad. Praise helps both partners focus on the best aspects of the work. And it just creates a positive workflow, which goes a very long way to improving the lonely frustrating world of writing.

I DO EVERYTHING, DAMN IT! In any partnership, there will be times you feel you are doing more than your share of the work. That's natural. Be prepared for it. Different writers work at different paces. A little patience will go a long way. Still, this is why deadlines are a good thing and should be spelled out in your agreement. If you are consistently finishing your Chapters on time, but then waiting weeks for your partner to complete their section, it may be more of a problem. There may just be incompatibilities in the work styles of you and your partner. But give it some time. There are growing pains in any partnership, so before you throw a fit, make sure your partner is truly slacking and you're not just impatient.

YOU DO EVERYTHING, DAMN IT! The corollary to the above problem is the fear that your partner is doing everything. They provide most of the plot. They volunteer themselves to do more of the writing. They want final say. This, of course, calls into question why they need a collaborator at all if they want to do it all. However, it could just be your perception. Your partner may genuinely be stepping in to help. They may be someone who is in a constant state of panic about the work; they're always frantic about production, about editing, about everything. Talk to them. Be clear that you want to contribute. You want your voice to be present in the finished product. And again, deadlines help. If you are meeting yours, you should keep your part of the project.

Now We're Ready To Collaborate. What Can We Expect?

PART 2: Here's the Good Stuff

Now that we've dealt with some of the problems you will face in collaboration—and thoroughly discouraged you—let's take up the topic of why collaboration is beneficial to your writing. And it is. All writers should expect to collaborate in some way in the process of their career. You will collaborate every day with your editor, your publicist, your beta readers, etc. The ability to recognize its benefits and embrace them will aid you in the long run.

STRENGTHS AND WEAKNESS: DESPITE WHAT YOUR MOTHER TOLD YOU, YOU AREN'T GOOD AT EVERYTHING. Like all people, you have strengths and weaknesses. When collaboration works best, the partners bring different strengths to the table. When we first began writing, Susan was better at establishing character and understanding when emotional beats were needed. Clay was better at plotting and world building. In fact, we each approached projects differently. Susan wrote from the character out. Clay wrote from the concept in. Susan's approach could lead to interesting characters who wandered around not doing interesting things. Clay's style created a solid premise, but contained placeholder characters whose sole task seemed to be pushing plot points from page to page. The joining of these two styles created a more complete style, compelling characters propelled by big issues.

The advantage of having access to skills beyond your own also allows you to attempt projects or blend genre elements you might have avoided. Clay now has written books that thrive on strong relationships, and Susan has written deft political intrigue. These are not areas we would have attempted before, at least not as successfully. So perhaps the most obvious advantage of collaboration is an instant addition of skills not your own. Suddenly you have a masterful writer of fight scenes to add to your own love of drawing room dialogue. Perhaps your partner has an intrinsic ability to know when a scene is done while you tend to run on out of a sense of realism.

That's why the best collaborations come from writers with differences. If you both have the same strengths, it might be more difficult to realize the greatest value of your partnership. On the other hand, too much difference can also create problems. If you love splatterpunk horror and your partner wants to write regency romance, there might not be a lot of crossover there (give it a shot, though—splatteregency!™).

LEARNING NEW SKILLS: NOW YOU ARE THE STUDENT AND I AM THE MASTER. Learn new stuff! Don't just leave your partner to their expertise. Learn what they know. Absorb it. Use it. For example, when we first started, Clay was better at action because it was more plot-based. Susan, however, took her character skills, learned how to drive and control their movements, added her superior descriptive talents, and now her fight/action sequences are far better than Clay's. And conversely, Clay has learned little character touches—a look, a gesture, a momentary pause—and when blended with his natural love of dialogue, his characters are not just the smart-asses they used to be. No, they're far stronger and more loveable than when he wrote solo.

You should always be absorbing your partner's strengths and making them your own. It's an extension of a writer's love of research (most writers love research anyway). How can you not read your partner's superior action sequences and think "How did she do that?" and "How can I do that?" So learn! You don't have to get it from a book on writing or a seminar at a conference. It's right there in front of you. There's no excuse for not getting better. And soon you won't have to insert little notes in the manuscript for your partner like "put something funny here" or "fix this fight."

IDEAS: TWO MINDS CAN BE BETTER THAN ONE. Brainstorming can be a wonderful, chaotic, organic thing. Throwing out ideas and shooting them down. Latching onto a concept and developing it, adding layers and attachments, building it first one way and then another before realizing it doesn't work and then moving on to the next idea. With a writing partner, you always have someone to bounce ideas off. You don't have to wait for your next writing group meeting. You don't have to annoy your husband/wife/brother/mom/ stranger-at-the-bus-stop for the millionth time until finally they all start hiding when they see you coming. Brainstorming with someone who is invested in the project always is more useful than with someone who is trying to see the TV over your shoulder while you're explaining your problem resolving the issue of Steve's mysterious birthmark.

INCREASED PRODUCTION: WHAT IS THE SOUND OF FOUR HANDS TYPING. It isn't always true that multiple writers work faster than a solo writer, but the odds are good that it will be. It's certainly possible that each partner is a slow writer who churns out words at a glacial pace. At the very least, then, there are two glacial writers working at the same time, which means you're creating more words than one glacial writer. So that's good. Isn't it?

Plus, having a partner gives you the opportunity for multi-tasking. One partner can be researching while the other is plotting or writing. One partner can be editing earlier chapters while the other is finishing a first draft of the book. One partner can be writing while the other is at the grocery store. The minor and major catastrophes of life don't have to bring production to halt.

COMMUNICATION (PART I): I'M THINKING WE SHOULD KILL STEVE IN CHAPTER 5...HEY, YOU MISSED THE EXIT. Collaboration gives you something to talk about with your partner, something creative, something you're both passionate about, and something that you both want to go well. The amount of communication you experience depends on how close you are to your partner, physically anyway. For example, we're married and we live in the same house. No day passes that we don't talk about whatever project we're working on. Sometimes we talk about it ad nauseum. And there are actually times when one or the other of us will get tired of it. If so, we simply say, "Could we please have dinner without talking about blood-drinking gorillas tonight?" The other should comply, if they don't want to wear the meatloaf, that is. But no matter where you each live, there is nothing better than to be able to walk in the next room or pick up the phone or fire off an email or text or Skype and engage in a conversation about a creative endeavor with someone who is just as psyched about it as you are.

COMMUNICATION (PART 2): YOU KILLED STEVE IN CHAPTER 5? I HAVE HIM MARRYING BARBARA IN CHAPTER 12? Are you the strong silent type? That schtick won't work with a writing partner. Failing to communicate is a disaster waiting to happen. There's no excuse for not communicating. There are too many problems that can occur down the road if partners don't share information. No matter how hidebound you are about your meticulous outline, things will change during the writing. There are always new ideas that occur that can make the book better. If you don't communicate with your partner, aside from the loss of brainstorming advantages and the pleasures of conversation, you could wander off down a path that your partner is not on. And suddenly you are in essence writing a different book. That's bad.

HOW TO COLLABORATE

Now that we've discussed some of the problems you will face and the benefits you should embrace when collaborating with a writing partner, let's talk nuts and bolts. Much of it is a matter of personal tastes. Different writers work in different ways, and collaboration doesn't change most of that. None of this will be gospel and there will be plenty of methods we don't address, but we will give you a starting point.

Tools of Your Trade: If it ain't broke, don't fix it. Continue to write however you write best. Collaborating doesn't mean that when it comes time to get words on paper, you and your partner sit in a room together while one of you dictates and the other one types like in those old movies where a composer and a lyricist pound out a hit Broadway song together. Some writing teams work that way, but most don't. The act of writing is a solitary endeavor, and it remains so even when working with a partner.

Some writers work in the morning, some in the evening, some any time they get a minute. Some writers set a schedule for themselves; they have to write 1000 words per day no matter what. Others write as much as they can; one day it might be 100 words, but the next day could be 5000. Do what works best for you as a writer, whether you were collaborating or not, as long as you can meet your obligations, of course.

For example, Clay usually writes first drafts on a yellow legal pad with a pen. Yes, you heard it. He writes longhand. When he writes in a coffee shop, people with their iMacs and tablets stare at him as if he is chipping cuneiform into a stone tablet. But he doesn't care because it's how he is most comfortable writing. Parts of the first draft of this chapter were written down on a sheet of paper with a pen. That's right, just like Voltaire would've written it! Susan, on the other hand, tends to compose on-screen, editing as she goes. None of that matters as long as the pages get written.

A Single Voice: Keep writing until it doesn't sound like you. This is one of the trickiest parts of collaboration to master. When you write as a team, you no longer write as yourself. You are a new author, a whole different entity. We are not Clay Griffith and Susan Griffith. We are Clay and Susan

Griffith, and we write differently than either of us. As a solo writer, Clay is very terse. Light on descriptions and adjectives. Simple direct sentences. Stories are carried by dialogue. Susan writes more descriptively, using longer passages with a plethora of beautiful adjectives and adverbs, allowing her stories to be carried by internal monologues. Clay and Susan try to balance their tendencies and meet in the middle.

A good example of how we blend our styles is our use of emotional tags to character action or dialogue. Clay writes a lot of he said/she said. Susan always adds emotional descriptors to his spare text. Clay argues back that the reader will supply the emotion thanks to the context of the scene or the dialogue spoken, and that too many emotional descriptions break up the pacing. Susan argues that, like a screenplay, sometimes the right emotion on the page helps the actor shows the emotion. Therefore, it's up to the writer to be the actor as well as the writer. So Clay tries to add more emotional cues to his writing, despite it being against his nature, but not nearly as many as Susan would have in her solo writing. Ultimately our goal (and your goal) is for someone to read our work, someone who knows us each individually, and say they can't tell who wrote what.

So how do you do that? You work like crazy at it. There are two ways we approach projects, depending on size. For a small piece, such as a short story or comic book script, one of us will write a complete first draft and then hand it to the other for editing. It might go back and forth a few times.

For a larger project, such as a novel, the process is more involved. First, we plot the book in as much detail as possible. We try to break the outline down on a chapter-by-chapter level. This involves a lot of dinners and coffee talking over plot ideas. It makes for a lot of "How about if…" and "It would be good if we could…" as well as plenty of "No, I don't like that because…" (Good.) and "Are you kidding me? That sucks." (Bad.)

Of course we know that no matter how detailed we make

the plot, it might come unraveled as we work and we'll have to re-plot, sometimes over and over. There will always be the dreaded appearance of your partner in your office door with a thoughtful look on their face as they say, "You know, I was thinking…." And you might find their new idea is exactly the right way to go. Even if it requires throwing out pages or even chapters that have already been written. As always, it's better to have a story that is the best you can deliver than be a slave to your plot or worry too much about protecting material you've worked hard on. Sometimes, you just have to be cruel and spike that emotional chapter about Steve falling in love with a talking balloon that one day develops a slow leak and he has to watch helplessly as it deflates, squealing his name in a tiny helium voice. Sorry, that's got to go.

Once we have an outline, we divide up the book, usually in multi-chapter chunks. We might try to separate the writing based on material that is more in our comfort zone. Clay might do the scenes that are heavily political or smart-ass driven. Susan handles intimacy and fist fights. But we each do a little of everything. After we are fairly satisfied with our drafts, we hand the chapters over for editing. We each alter the language a bit so it comes out sounding like *us* rather than either Clay or Susan.

We proceed through the project in stages. We don't each write all of our chapters for the entire book before showing them to our partner, or reading our partner's work. We might work our way through chapters 1-10 and then start editing each other before moving on to chapter 11-20. It's important to check for redundancy and contradictions. If Clay mentions Steve's love of ice cream in chapter 3, there's no need for Susan's reference to it in chapter 8 (unless hers is better, then cut the ice cream from 3). See how tricky? We also want to see what little character elements each of us are putting in, what nice dialogue bits might be in there, so we can use them as motifs throughout the book, sprinkling them in as call-backs to create texture. Or, conversely, we may want to cut them if the other author disagrees with that interpretation of a character.

And so we work our way through the book, discussing and writing and re-writing and cutting and re-rewriting and blending our separate voices into one. After six books, numerous short stories, and lots of comics, we're pretty good at creating in a joint style from the beginning.

The blending of partner's voices takes time and effort, but it is imminently doable. You have to redirect a large part of your ego toward a joint goal. You can't think "My writing is so much better than theirs; they should write more like me." If you don't truly think your partner's writing is superior or equal to yours, you probably won't collaborate long.

DISTANCE: ACROSS THE TABLE OR AROUND THE WORLD. Sometimes the proximity of your collaborator isn't really a choice. Unless you are married, it's unlikely you will be in the same house as your partner at all times. Never fret though, you can still manage successful collaborations from any distance. It's just that the farther apart you are, the more planning and tools you will need.

When we run up against a problem, we can deal with it instantaneously. We stop writing, find the other person and say, "We have a problem. Stop what you're doing until you agree with me." It usually works pretty well, unless one of us is raiding in Warcraft. Plus, our proximity prevents hours or days of nervous frustration worrying about the problem and how it's going to get fixed, or what you should do until it gets fixed.

Of course with texting and Skyping and emails and even the old telephone, that sort of immediate connection with your partner is still possible even if you're in New York and they are in Abu Dhabi. We prefer face-to-face because we still have a tendency to misunderstand one another (that LISTEN lesson is a hard one!), and it's easier to hash that out in person across the kitchen rather than through a long train of increasingly convoluted emails. But that's us. Other partners work just fine with written or distant communication. So if you want to partner up with someone far away, don't let the far away part of the equation stop you.

FILE SHARING: ARE YOU WORKING ON CHAPTER 12? BECAUSE I THOUGHT I WAS. How you actually move work back and forth between partners is, again, up to you. There are many ways to approach the issue. You can have each partner work on a particular file independently and then hand it off, or you can use a file sharing system. We maintain individual control of files. For example, if Clay writes chapter 12 and then hands it to Susan for editing, she controls that file at that point. He can no longer touch it until she hands it back to him. It's not a foolproof system as we have had instances where we were both working on the same material at the same time without realizing it, or waiting for the other partner to return an edited file, while the partner had no idea they even had it in their control. "I've got the gorilla fight chapter?! I thought you had that!!" But those failings are more a symptom of a breakdown in communication (communication is really important, see above!) than it is a problem with the system itself. It has served us for multiple novels and comics, and we'll keep using it.

The other system is one that we have never used, i.e. file sharing and real-time collaboration, but it's certainly doable and there are many different systems to use. There are products that allow you and your partner to work on a document that sits in a neutral site, usually the cloud, so you can both access it equally all the time. Some of the products allow you both to work on the document at the same time, something that seems more useful to business documents, but if that's a collaboration style you wish to adopt, you may find them useful. Many of them may also have limitations in terms of the size of documents, so may or may not be convenient for large projects like a novel.

The most common file sharing service is probably Google docs. It's part of the Google online empire of services and products. There are many others such as Sharepoint and SkyDox. Products such as Etherpad, Agilewords, or Thinkfree are notable for real-time collaboration. We don't recommend any of these products or services over any others, nor do we pretend to trumpet their usefulness, because we have never used them. But, again, depending on how you and your partner want to structure your collaboration style, they may serve you well.

While we don't advocate any software or products over others, we do think it's wise for you to use the same programs to minimize problems with sharing and formatting. If you're both going over a final manuscript, it's good that when one of you says "We need to change *kiss* on page 213 line 7 to *kill*" that you both are looking at the same *kiss*. We both use Word for writing, and sometimes Scrivener for organizing plots. It might be possible that we would use Scrivener for more than just plotting, but Clay is too old-fashioned and doesn't adapt well to newfangled ideas. (Remember the legal pad? Pen? Yeah, that.)

MAKE A SYSTEM AND STICK TO IT: IS YOUR CHAPTER 12.1-3 THE SAME AS MY CHAPTER 12B+2? The idea of consistency is important in so many ways, but here we're talking about organizational and "bookkeeping" type stuff. For example, when you name files, both of you should use the same system. This is particularly important if you pass material back and forth the way we do. We might go through 10 or more versions and even alternate versions of some chapters. Make sure both partners are using the same naming conventions to denote a new version. There is nothing worse than getting deep into a project and having one partner say, "Wait a minute, what happened to chapter 12? Steve is supposed to kill the Komodo dragon with the laser gun."

"Are you high? Steve has always killed the Komodo dragon with a spear gun."

"No. I wrote a laser gun scene six months ago. It was the best scene in the book. I sent it to you as ver.12xaltb."

"Oh yeah, I had no idea what it was. So I deleted it and used my original Chap.12/7.5."

"God dammit! I hate you!"

"Fine! Then go write a book with your old boyfriend. Oh that's right, he's in jail!"[17]

And so on. You can see how difficult that could be, right? So take a few minutes and set up a system you can both agree on.

Conclusion:
If you can write together, you can probably be married.

As we said at the beginning, not everyone can collaborate in writing. Some people just don't want to. They never want to surrender their independence, or compromise their personal vision. And that's fine. For those of you who do want to work with a partner, however, remember that a good marriage is a metaphor for good collaboration in writing. Here are two things you should remember.

TRUST. You must ultimately trust your partner. You must believe they know what they're talking about, that their talent is strong and their intentions are good. You must know they will do their work, that they are committed. And most of all, you must trust that they want what's best for the project, not necessarily what's best for them. When they make a cut or an edit, you have to know that they're doing it because they

---

17 *No one's ex-boyfriend is in jail.*

believe it makes the work better, not because they're trying to preserve or highlight their own contribution. While we recommend that you and your collaborator create a contract to lay out the expectations and limits of your partnership, no agreement can replace trust at the heart of a collaboration.

VALUE YOUR PARTNER'S CONTRIBUTION. Remember, your partner is a writer, and presumably a good writer. You must love their work. You must see the worth of working together. When you talk to others, your partner should always be a better writer. You must believe that your writing isn't as good solo as it is together.

After all, if you're not producing better work together, why collaborate?

CHAPTER 12

The Home Field Disadvantage

Leah Petersen

If you're reading this book, you know that writing is a craft, a technical exercise, a skill that can be acquired. But behind every well-crafted story is a person, an emotional being, and, because of that, writing can be a brutal game. We bring ourselves to these stories, we put our hearts and souls into them and that's what makes them great.

We also live in the real world. Unless we manage to hide our passion for writing from everyone we know and love, we're going to encounter pushback in real life.

I know whereof I speak. I live in a conservative Christian part of the country surrounded by my conservative Christian family and I write about gay people. As I myself am a straight woman with two kids, who ostensibly fits into the stereotype of the area, it comes as a shock to some that I write things that are often roundly condemned here.

Better authors than me have faced similar challenges. Harper Lee was a woman living in the deep South at the height of the Civil Rights movement when she wrote *To Kill a Mockingbird*, which staunchly condemned racial discrimination. You think that didn't get a few panties in a bunch? Oh yeah.

In 1966, Lee wrote a letter to the editor in response to the attempts of a Richmond, Virginia area school board to ban *To Kill a Mockingbird* as "immoral literature":

"Recently I have received echoes down this way of the Hanover County School Board's activities, and what I've heard makes me wonder if any of its members can read.

"Surely it is plain to the simplest intelligence that *To Kill a Mockingbird* spells out in words of seldom more than two syllables a code of honor and conduct, Christian in its ethic, that is the heritage of all Southerners. To hear that the novel is 'immoral' has made me count the years between now and 1984, for I have yet to come across a better example of doublethink.

"I feel, however, that the problem is one of illiteracy, not Marxism. Therefore I enclose a small contribution to the Beadle Bumble Fund that I hope will be used to enroll the Hanover County School Board in any first grade of its choice."

I think I'm in love.

Salman Rushdie's fourth book, *The Satanic Verses*, prompted violent protests around the world, even earned him a fatwa from the Supreme Leader of Iran. How's that for a negative reaction?

I approached my own journey into the world of published-author-of-probably-not-popular-subject-matter with the hopes that I could mostly keep the subject of my writing under the radar at home, and connect through the Internet with people who would actually want to read what I'd written. I resigned myself to the fact that my mother would never read my book. I decided to let it not be a part of my Real Life.

I did eventually tell my extended family, as my book release date approached, that I had a book coming out with gay people in it. This is not a good thing where I live. They were not happy, but in the interest of preserving the peace, we all said little about it and proceeded to pretend we'd never had that conversation. Months later one of them came up to me and said, "So-and-so other relative told me you she read your book and it was really good! Why didn't you tell me you had a book like that out there?" I paused, considered, and then replied, "I did. It's the one with the gay people in it." Cue crickets.

So, I suppose, by that reckoning a book with gay people in it can't be good—at least around here.

So, how about you? Are you writing something on the edge, controversial, even shocking? What about something that won't faze the rest of the world but will scandalize the people in your day-to-day life?

You don't have to be writing erotica or grimdark to find yourself in that position, because behind every story is a message. The frustrating part is, you can't control that message. Oh, that's not to say that you have no influence over what a reader takes away from your writing. It's hard to interpret a socialist message out of *Atlas Shrugged*, or a religious orthodox message from *Candide*. Someone will manage it, but that's outside the scope of this writing.

The one constant, though, is that every reader is a person, and they'll bring themselves to your writing just as you did when writing it. That means sometimes you're going to piss them off. That means sometimes you're going to piss a lot of them off, including the people you know. You can't control that, short of not letting your writing see the light of day.

This doesn't just apply to writing about controversial things. You could be writing romances while surrounded with literary fiction snobs. Or science fiction among a population that thinks sci-fi is only for losers still living in mom's basement. Or fantasy around people who think that's the devil's way to snare children.

So, what happens when your writing isn't exactly what those around you are…comfortable with?

Wouldn't it be great if you could just hide? Sorry, the days of the anonymous writer are gone. Sure there are pen names, and a lot of us use them. A nom de plume can be a great way to distance your "real" life from the fame—and sometimes infamy—of your writing life. It can also help you separate your "main" writer persona from the things you might write that your standard readership isn't looking for. The literary fiction writer who gets a little extra money on the side from writing robot porn is doing this. You may too. You may even decide that, even though you're writing the modern day *Little House on the Prairie*, putting your real name out there isn't something you're interested in doing.

When I had a shiny new completed novel of my very own and set out to find a publisher for it, at first I considered a pen name. To me it sounded like a great way to avoid all the flak I'd get from the community, my family, acquaintances and friends who might see my name on the Internet. In other words, I was afraid to own what I'd written.

I don't think it was cowardly to seriously consider a very practical way to try to avoid the real life consequences of my controversial subject matter. Do it if that's the right thing for you. In the end, though, I decided not to. Why?

For starters, even behind a pen name, we'll never be truly anonymous the way writers of yesteryear could be. Already scholars have figured out who all of them were. In our Information Age, with the ubiquity and omniscience of the Internet, you'll have about 5.5 seconds of true anonymity before the thirteen-year-old next door figures out the neighbor lady is the one who wrote "that book."

There was also the simple reason that I didn't think I could pull it off. I'm not the kind of reserved person who can keep a big part of my life completely out of my day-to-day interactions. I can't *not* talk about it to friends and family, even if I know their reactions may be less than supportive. If the pen name wasn't going to be an effective place to hide then, for me, it would just be a hassle.

There's also the consideration, which I began to understand as I sought an agent and a publisher, that trying to remain anonymous behind a pen name makes marketing and networking *really* difficult. Do you use your real name with your fellow authors when you meet them at conventions, or will you live your pen name everywhere you go in the writing community? We meet a lot of people at conventions. Will they remember that Ann Smith that they met and liked goes by the pen name D.P. Netherweave? How will you handle book signings or other public events? Interviews? Guest appearances? The marketing angle is important, and we'll get more into that later.

Because before you can decide if a pen name is right for you, let's get into the potential reasons why you might choose one, or not. What factors will come into consideration?

You may face outright opposition. Every town has that one person, or several, who has no brain-to-mouth filter, or worse, who doesn't care who they hurt on their righteous crusade against...whatever. Perhaps this person has a large platform or a lot of local influence. Maybe they're in your family. Use Facebook? Have fun with some of the characters on there who think the thin protection of a computer monitor gives them license to say whatever they want.

Passive hostility is another likely scenario. Coworkers, family members, even casual acquaintances may express their disapproval in this fun and not-at-all-frustrating way. Again, Facebook and Twitter are new and exciting places for people to play out their passive aggression. Ready the unfriend button if necessary.

Self-doubt is an insidious challenge you might face. Maybe you can't handle the opposition? Is your work really good enough to make all this worth it? What if the naysayers are right? You can be your own worst enemy.

Fear's even worse. What if you make a fool of yourself? What if your outright opponents make you look ridiculous in front of people whose opinion you value? What if the passive-aggression makes other people laugh at you? What if your book is shredded in the reviews and now you've ruined your life for nothing?

Scared yet? Don't be.

In some ways, this just goes back to that old issue of peer pressure, and Being Different. It's also an interesting conundrum for the otherwise-normal-by-local-standards writer. Unlike those who *have* to live their Otherness, who cannot hide how they are not Just Like Everyone Else, some of us really do have the chance to sit back and pretend to be just one of the gang. That may even be why we started writing: a creative outlet for all the things inside of us that didn't fit into the happy little social mold. Now, we're going to put it out there, and People are Going to Find Out.

It's not easy. Nothing about writing is. You'll pour your time and energy into honing your craft, then you'll pour your heart and soul into that manuscript until you're ready to put it out there for the world to see, and then you'll go all in when your name and your passion hit the internets.

When it came down to it, I really didn't get much reaction at all, besides the trusty Ignore Things that Make Us Uncomfortable. But finally a family member went there, telling us all how the Bible condemns homosexuality, blah, blah, so on and so forth. You've heard the speech. Nothing hostile, the sort of encounter that could be handled with a polite nod and then moving on.

Maybe some people can make that work, but I'm not one of them. I'm not good at compartmentalizing or hiding who I am and I don't have a lot of success at holding my tongue. Thankfully, I'm also forceful enough—in that Southern Belle kind of way, when necessary—that I can usually state my fervent opposition and then pretend they intended to end the conversation there and simply move on to another topic. Therefore I got to say my piece and then we talked about food or the weather or something. Your mileage may vary.

How do you handle it when it's your turn? Are you ready? What will you tell the people most important to you? Do you tell your mom all about it, expecting her to read and love your work and brag about it to all her friends? Can you be content will simply telling her about it, accepting vague praise for your accomplishment, and then have her flat-out refuse to read it and never speak of it to anyone? How do you manage that sort of thing long term, if you're not planning to move out of the country and change your phone number?

What if the best happens and you get big? Really big? Now you're on Good Morning America and The Daily Show. Your name is in magazines, newspapers, and all over the Internet. That's great for book sales and for your bank account. How is it going to affect your personal life?

What about your partner? She has family too. And coworkers, friends. Have you talked to her about how this will affect both of you?

What about your kids? How do they feel about the message you're sending? How do they want to deal with it among their friends and schoolmates? How will you help them?

The good news with kids is that they tend to be a lot less judgmental than adults. In my own experience, my kids get far less hassle from their peers than I do. And they're old enough to form their own opinions. My son tends to shrug it off to his friends in that "parents are always embarrassing" kind of way. My daughter, for better or for worse, has picked up on the prevailing attitude among our family and decided she doesn't approve of my "gay books" anyway. So when people criticize, she has no real incentive to care. Prepare to deal with something like that. And take into account their ages (this is all so much easier if they can't talk yet), personalities, and needs.

The only real thing you can do is prepare yourself. Decide ahead of time what and how much you will tell and to whom. Then be prepared for them to shock you, sometimes in a good way.

If you've decided already to be as incognito as possible, you'll mostly avoid uncomfortable situations. When you can't, and someone does become aware of what you've written and doesn't like what you say, you might simply refuse to listen to or engage them.

But you should still think about how you'll respond when an issue arises. Plan for how that will vary depending on who brings it up. Your response to your grandma getting in your face and loudly disapproving will be different than your response to the local evangelist doing the exact same thing. Be prepared for the passive aggression, and for people important to you to simply ignore the work that means so much to you.

There are certainly different ways to handle the disapproval and opposition. You can always fall back on the tried and true ignore, or the tried but often frustrating in-your-face, loud-and-proud response. In my experience, the best approach for me has been to have a simple, respectful response to their disapproval and then leave. Something along the lines of "I hear your concerns but I don't agree, also I understand what you're saying and I don't care." Maybe leave off the "don't care" part, though admittedly that's fun in the right situation.

Take heart, you are not in this alone.

Even as it's the thing that will "out" you, the Internet is also the thing that can save you. Meet people there who aren't bothered by the themes you write about. More important, meet people there who are *moved* by the things you write about, who are passionate about them, the people whose lives you changed by tackling that tough issue and doing it well. You can also connect with the people who live that reality.

Those people are your saviors. Eventually you'll realize they're *why* you're doing this, even if you didn't know that when you started out. As solitary and isolating as writing can feel sometimes, ultimately it's a way to connect with others, it's a shared experience, a lifeline. That first email you get telling you what a difference your book made in someone's life, that first person who comes up to you at a convention and can't stop talking about what your book means to them, that first gushing review? Those things may not be why you did this, but they're why you'll keep doing it.

We don't put our work out there because we want to hide. If that was the case, we'd keep it on the hard drive, or delete the file when it was finished. Let the people you hoped to reach when you released your baby into the world be the people who hold you up when you feel like you're falling. They may not be able to have your back when someone at the grocery store or the office doesn't take well to where you've taken your creative genius, but they can be a shoulder to cry on, or a pick-me-up afterward.

You can also rely on your fellow authors. Some have been through just what you're going through. They can provide practical help and support. Search online for some of your favorite authors. Chances are, one or two of them actively blog or tweet. Following them and participating in the conversation is a great way to meet others like you. Join the authors' association specific to what you write. The Society of Children's Book Writers and Illustrators (SCBWI) is the go-to group for YA authors. A side benefit of meeting other authors is that some will be and can help you understand the people and situations and themes you're trying to write about but have no personal experience with.

But let's leave behind the touchy-feely for a moment. There are practical considerations too. How do you plan to approach marketing? Now that you've decided how you're going to handle the pushback, you'll want to make sure you earn it, and that's by selling a lot of books. What are some things even those of us not in the middle of a modern, cosmopolitan area can do?

Just to start the list, there's your online spaces: Facebook, Goodreads, Twitter, your blog. There's in-person marketing, even if it's not feasible in your immediate area. And there are conventions you can attend to meet fans and sell books.

So much of book selling these days is selling yourself and your brand. You pull a reader in with creative marketing and outreach on the internet and everywhere else. Then you keep them because they love your books and will buy the next one you publish. They're following the name. Going back to the topic above, here's where using a pen name can become tricky, but not an insurmountable obstacle. Everything you do in marketing, whether behind a screen or in person, will need to be as the name you write under. Your face will be out there too. So if you're planning on remaining anonymous behind a pen name, keep that in mind.

Most authors have the opportunity to do a lot of in-person marketing in their own area. Readings and signings at local restaurants and bookstores can be an effective and fun way to promote yourself and your book. Not so much if the businesses in your area don't want to promote or be associated with "one of *those* books." The only local bookstore in my area is a Christian bookstore. I didn't even bother to ask if they wanted to host a signing for my gay sci-fi. If you're in a similar situation, you may find yourself equally stymied in your marketing efforts.

That's okay, there's hope! Part of why we end up being in situations where we're so different from our neighbors is because the world has gotten very small. Not just the passive exposure of TV and radio, or even the very active but expensive access to travel almost anywhere in the world. The Internet is where we find new things, expand our horizons, open our minds. That's no doubt part of why you're even reading this Chapter. It's how you came to the place where you were ready to challenge the worldview you were raised with, or that your neighbors hold to.

The Internet is one of your most powerful marketing tools. Facebook pages, blogs, Twitter, Goodreads. You'll find your readers and your readers will find you.

Twitter is free, and it's a great place, not only to market your books, but to meet your fellow authors and fans. But be careful. The biggest thing you need to remember about Twitter is this: Don't be annoying. Twitter is a place to have a conversation and connect. Spamming is very bad and will hurt you far more than it will help you. Of course you can and should talk about your book. But talk about other people's books too, and other things. Be someone people want to follow.

You can run ads on Facebook and Goodreads, or do giveaways. Shop around, and do your research. Not all ads are equal. Facebook's new way of prioritizing what posts people see can put a huge dent in the impact an ad there may have for you, but it can reach a wider audience. Goodreads ads will have a smaller audience but they will all be readers, and you can target people who read in your genre. Giveaways on your blog will only cost you the price of the book you're giving away. However, you're reaching only your current blog audience and those you manage to drive there by advertising the giveaways on Twitter, and elsewhere online.

Blog tours don't care where you live, and they reach out to people who don't share your neighbors' prejudices. If you've been doing your job pre-launch, you've been online researching and networking and you've met a lot of other authors, reviewers, and book bloggers ahead of the release. You can set up your own blog tour among them. When you write your blog posts, your experiences in real life can provide topics to start conversations online. If you don't have the contacts or the time to build a blog tour of your own, there are many places online offering that service. Most of them are genre specific, or offer genre specific packages. Make sure you're investing your money to put your books in front of the right audience.

And you can still connect with your readers in person. You can go to fan and genre conventions. You'll meet readers and network with authors who can do amazing things for your career or just be there to support you and help you improve your craft.

Conventions are an excellent way to promote yourself and your books. But how do you find the one that's right for you? This one's especially important because, unlike blog tours, these always cost money. That's especially true if you don't live in or near a big city where the conventions come to you. So it's important to find the right one. And that doesn't always mean the closest.

Balance the cost of the convention registration, the cost of the hotel and airfare if applicable, against the potential benefit of the convention itself. Large conventions will be more expensive, and you'll be competing for attention against a lot of other people. As a new author, you'll be less likely to get any of the spotlight or meet the important people.

That said, there is more than one definition of benefit, attention, and important. The up-and-comers may be much more valuable contacts for you than the ones who are big names now. There's no guarantee you won't get attention from the people with the most influence. There are too many factors that go into something like that. (As a don't-try-this-at-home example, I broke my foot at a World Fantasy Convention and one of the guests of honor stopped by to talk to poor pathetic me sitting there with my broken foot. It's probably too embarrassing to mention the midlist author who offered to help me get to the bathroom, which I had to take him up on.)

Small conventions have their benefit too, and in my personal opinion and experience, for a new author they're the best investment. At a small, focused con, you'll likely be able to participate on panels. You'll have less competition for attention in the dealers room and with the guest of honor. You can meet organizers and influential fans who can help you advance your career. And you'll get more opportunity to meet your fans, both current fans and the ones who will be your fans now that they've discovered you. All these things are really good for the new author and don't preclude becoming a bigger fish in the pond next go-round. In fact, they'll make that more likely.

Now that you've narrowed it down to what size convention you're going to attend, which one among all the offerings do you pick? The wrong convention is at best a waste of money, at worst it may lead you to focus on all the wrong things for you and the genre you write in. Here's where your networking will be invaluable. Talk to your fellow authors, your editor, your fans. What have their experiences been? Where will they be? That's where you need to go.

So in the space of this chapter we've gone from the emotional and social impact of your writing in your personal life, to how you can make it impact you—and others—in much bigger ways. This wasn't a scare-you-straight lecture but a pep talk. You aren't alone, and you can do this.

Writing's never easy. From that first word to the last book sold. But it *can* be done and it *is* worth it. Welcome to this crazy thing we call being an author. It's a wild ride but you'll love it.

APPENDICES

Appendix A: Books Mentioned

Appendix B: Authors Mentioned

Appendix C: Glossary of Literary Devices

Literary devices are a collection of universal artistic structures that are frequently employed by writers. We have included a glossary of literary devices here as a reference aid. Browsing through them may spark ideas, or may put names to concepts whose names you hadn't known before.

ADAGE: a saying, often in metaphorical form, that embodies a common observation (*also: Aphorism*).

ALLEGORY: a story in which the characters and events are symbols that stand for ideas about human life or for a political or historical situation.

ALLUSION: a statement that refers to something without mentioning it directly.

ANACHRONISM: an error in chronology; especially a chronological misplacing of persons, events, objects, or cutoms in regard to each other.

ANADIPLOSIS: repetition of a prominent and usually the last word in one phrase or clause at the beginning of the next (as in "rely on his honor—honor such as his?").

ANAPHORA: repetition of a word or expression at the beginning of successive phrases, clauses, sentences, or verses especially for rhetorical or poetic effect. (Lincoln's "we cannot dedicate—we cannot consecrate—we cannot hallow—this ground").

ANTIMETABOLE: the repetition of words in successive clauses, but in transposed order (e.g., "I know what I like, and I like what I know"). It is similar to chiasmus although chiasmus does not use repetition of the same words or phrases.

APHORISM: a concise statement of a principle, truth, or sentiment (*also: Adage*).

APOPHASIS: A rhetorical device wherein the speaker or writer brings up a subject by denying that it should be brought up. (also Paralipsis, occupatio, paraleipsis, paralepsis, cataphasis).

APOSTROPHE: the addressing of a usually absent person or a usually personified thing rhetorically (Carlyle's "O Liberty, what things are done in thy name!").

ASSONANCE: the use of words that have the same or very similar vowel sounds near one another (as in "summer fun" and "rise high in the bright sky"); a repetition of vowels without a repetition of consonants, used as an alternate to rhyme in verse.

BATHOS: An abrupt transition in style from the exalted commonplace or from the somber to the absurd, producing a humorous effect. ("The ships hung in the sky in much the same way that bricks don't." – Douglas Adams, HHGTG).

BILDUNGSROMAN: a novel about the moral and psychological growth of the main character.

CACOPHONY: harsh or discordant sound; harshness in the sounds of words or phrases.

CARICATURE: exaggeration by means of often ludicrous distortion of parts or characteristics.

CHIASMUS: the figure of speech in which two or more clauses are related to each other through a reversal of structures in order to make a larger point; that is, the clauses display inverted parallelism. ("By day the frolic, and the dance by night". Samuel Johnson The Vanity of Human Wishes.)

CONCEIT: A figure of speech in which two noticeably unrelated objects are likened together with the help of similes or metaphors.

CONCESSION: a literary device whereby one acknowledges a point made by one's opponent. It indicates an understanding of the other party's concerns by demonstrating knowledge of the opposing position, in order to argue against those concerns and invalidate them. ("I know that joining the king's guard is dangerous and will take me away from my studies, but I'm already good with a sword and you've seen how I can read on horseback!").

CONNOTATION: an idea or feeling that a word invokes in addition to its literal or primary meaning.

DENOTATION: the literal or primary meaning of a word, in contrast to the feelings or ideas that the word suggests.

DEUS EX MACHINA: In ancient Greek and Roman drama, a god introduced into a play to resolve the entanglements of the plot. It has come to mean any artificial or improbable device which is introduced to resolve the difficulties of a plot.

DOPPELGANGER: a double of a living person and sometimes portrayed as a harbinger of bad luck.

DOUBLE ENTENDRE: a figure of speech in which a spoken phrase is devised to be understood in either of two ways.

ELLIPSIS: a series of dots that usually indicates an intentional omission of a word, sentence, or whole section from a text without altering its original meaning.

ELEGY: a mournful, melancholic or plaintive poem, especially a funeral song or a lament for the dead.

EPIGRAPH: a phrase, quotation, or poem that is set at the beginning of a document or component.

EPIPHANY: an illuminating realization or discovery, often resulting in a personal feeling of elation, awe, or wonder.

EPIPHORA: (*Also Epistrophe*) the repetition of the same word or words at the end of successive phrases, clauses or sentences.

EPISTROPHE: *See epiphora.*

ETHOS: a Greek word meaning "character" that is used to describe the guiding beliefs or ideals that characterize a community, nation, or ideology.

EUPHEMISM: a generally innocuous word or expression used in place of one that may be found offensive or suggest something unpleasant.

EXTENDED METAPHOR: when an author exploits a single metaphor or analogy at length through multiple linked vehicles, tenors, and grounds.

FLASH-FORWARD: a literary device in which the plot goes ahead of time i.e. a scene that interrupts and takes the narrative forward in time from the current time in a story.

FLASHBACK: interruptions that writers do to insert past events in order to provide background or context to the current events of a narrative.

FOIL: a character that shows qualities that are in contrast with the qualities of another character with the objective to highlight the traits of the other character.

FORESHADOWING: a literary device in which a writer gives an advance hint of what is to come later in the story.

HAMARTIA: a personal error in a protagonist's personality that brings about his tragic downfall in a tragedy.

HUBRIS: extreme pride and arrogance shown by a character that ultimately brings about his downfall.

HYPERBOLE: a figure of speech, which involves an exaggeration of ideas for the sake of emphasis

INFERENCE: a literary device used commonly in literature and in daily life where logical deductions are made based on premises assumed to be true.

INNUENDO: an indirect or a subtle observation about a thing or a person.

INVECTIVE: speech or writing that attacks, insults, or denounces a person, topic, or institution.

INVERSION: a literary technique in which the normal order of words is reversed in order to achieve a particular effect of emphasis or meter.

IRONY: a figure of speech in which words are used in such a way that their intended meaning is different from the actual meaning of the words.

JUXTAPOSITION: a literary technique in which two or more ideas, places, characters and their actions are placed side by side in a narrative or a poem for the purpose of developing comparisons and contrasts.

LITOTES: a figure of speech which employs an understatement by using double negatives or, in other words, positive statement is expressed by negating its opposite expressions.

MALAPROPISM: a use of an incorrect word in place of a similar sounding word that results in a nonsensical and humorous expression.

METAPHOR: a comparison between two unlike things that continues throughout a series of sentences in a paragraph or lines in a poem.

METONYMY: a figure of speech that replaces the name of a thing with the name of something else with which it is closely associated.

MOTIF: an object or idea that repeats itself throughout a literary work.

NEMESIS: literary device that refers to a situation of poetic justice where the good characters are rewarded for their virtues and the evil characters are punished for their vices.

NON SEQUITUR: literary devices which include the statements, sayings and conclusions that do not follow the fundamental principles of logic and reason.

ONOMATOPOEIA: a word which imitates the natural sounds of a thing.

OXYMORON: a figure of speech in which two opposite ideas are joined to create an effect.

PALINDROME: a word, number, sentence, or symbol. that is the same forwards as it is backwards.

PARADOX: a statement that appears to be self-contradictory or silly but may include a latent truth.

PERSONIFICATION: a figure of speech in which a thing, an idea or an animal is given human attributes. (such as wind whispering through trees).

POLYSYNDETON: a stylistic device in which coordinating conjunctions like "and", "or", "but" and "nor" (mostly and and or) which are used to join successive words, phrases or clauses in which these conjunctions might have been omitted.

PORTMANTEAU: a literary device in which two or more words are joined together to coin a new word. A portmanteau word is formed by blending parts of two or more words but it always refers to a single concept. (Blending breakfast and lunch to create "brunch").

RED HERRING: often used in detective or suspense novels, a change of subject or an irrelevant tangent that misleads readers or characters, or induces them to make false conclusions.

SYMBOLISM: the use of symbols to signify ideas and qualities by giving them symbolic meanings that are different from their literal sense.

SYNCOPE: the contraction or the shortening of a word by omitting sounds, syllables or letters from the middle of the word such as bos'n for the word boatswain. Similarly, ne'er for the word never and fo'c'sle for the word forecastle

SYNECDOCHE: a literary device in which a part of something represents the whole, or a whole represents a part. (The way "a suit" can be a term for a businessperson, or "wheels" can be used to refer to a car.)

SYNESTHESIA: a figurative use of words that draws a response from readers by creating an analogy that connects multiple senses.

TAUTOLOGY: the technique of repeating a word or idea within a phrase, sentence or paragraph to give an impression that the writer is providing extra information. ("There's nothing you can do that can't be done. There's nothing you can sing that can't be sung" - The Beatles).

THESIS: a powerful propelling force behind an entire work that guides it toward its ultimate purpose and the lesson it intends to instruct.

UNDERSTATEMENT: a figure of speech employed by writers or speakers to intentionally make a situation seem less important than it really is.

VERISIMILITUDE: likeness to the truth i.e. resemblance of a fictitious work to a real event even if it is a far-fetched one.

ZEUGMA: a figure of speech in which a word, usually a verb or an adjective, applies to more than one noun, blending together grammatically and logically different ideas. For instance, in a sentence "John lost his coat and his temper," the verb "lost" applies to both nouns, "coat" and "temper."

Appendix D: Recommended Reading from Chapter 6

HOLLY BLACK
The Coldest Girl in Coldtown
The Curse Workers Trilogy: White Cat, Red Glove, Black Heart
KENDARE BLAKE
Anna Dressed in Blood
Girl of Nightmares
LIBBA BRAY
Going Bovine
Gemma Doyle Trilogy: A Great & Terrible Beauty, The Sweet Far Thing & Rebel Angels
RACHEL CAINE
The Morganville Vampires Series
SUZANNE COLLINS
The Hunger Games Trilogy: The Hunger Games, Catching Fire & Mockingjay
SARAH BETH DURST
Drink, Slay, Love
TESSA GRATTON
Blood Magic (The Blood Journals)
JOHN GREEN
The Fault in our Stars
Looking for Alaska
DAVID LEVITHAN
Everyday
Boy Meets Boy

JOHN MARSDEN
Tomorrow When the War Began Series
The Ellie Chronicles Series

LISH MCBRIDE
Hold Me Closer, Necromancer
Necromancing the Stone

RUTA SEPETYS
Between Shades of Gray
Out of the Easy

MAGGIE STIEFVATER
Shiver Trilogy: Shiver, Linger & Forever
The Scorpio Races
The Raven Cycle (Expected Quartet): The Raven Boys, The Dream Thieves, & Blue Lily, Lily Blue
Ballad & Lament

LAINI TAYLOR
Daughter of Smoke & Bone
Days of Blood & Starlight
Dreams of Gods & Monsters

CAT WINTERS
In the Shadow of Blackbirds

ELIZABETH WEIN
Code Name Verity
Rose Under Fire

BRENNA YOVANOFF
The Replacement
The Space Between
Paper Valentine
Fiendish

ABOUT THE CONTRIBUTORS

Leah Bobet

Leah Bobet's first novel, *Above*, was nominated for the Andre Norton Award for Young Adult Science Fiction and Fantasy and the Prix Aurora Award for Best Young Adult Novel – English, and her short fiction has appeared in a variety of Year's Best anthologies. She lives in Toronto, Ontario, where she edits Ideomancer Speculative Fiction, picks urban apple trees, and works as a bookseller and civic engagement activist. Her second novel, *On Roadstead Farm*—a literary dustbowl fantasy where things blow up—is forthcoming from Clarion Books/Houghton Mifflin Harcourt. For more, visit her at www.leahbobet.com.

Fanny Valentine Darling

Fanny Valentine Darling lives and writes young adult urban fantasy in a small town in Northern California. She shares her home with her husband and daughter. Find her on the web at: fannydarling.com.

Deby Fredericks

Deby Fredericks has been a writer all her life, but thought of it as just a fun hobby until the late 1990s. She made her first sale, a children's poem, in 2000. Fredericks has four fantasy novels out through two small presses. The latest is *The Seven Exalted Orders*, released by Sky Warrior in 2012. Her children's stories and poems have appeared in magazines such as Boys' Life, Babybug, Ladybug, and a few anthologies. In the past, she served as Assistant Regional Advisor for the Inland Northwest Region of the Society of Children's Book Writers and Illustrators, International (SCBWI). Currently she is a children's editor with Sky Warrior.

Clay and Susan Griffith

Clay and Susan Griffith are a married couple who have written and published together for more than a decade. Their credits not only include two novels for Bantam Doubleday Dell in the mid-1990s and another novel for Pinnacle Entertainment Group in 2002, but also the Vampire Empire series for Pyr Books. They have numerous short stories published in many anthologies, some featuring noted genre characters like Kolchak the Night Stalker and The Phantom. They've also written scripts for television and published graphic novels. Visit them online at clayandsusangriffith.blogspot.com.

Gabrielle Harbowy

Gabrielle Harbowy is an editor for such diverse SF/F publishers as Pyr and Circlet Press. She is the managing editor at Dragon Moon Press and a submissions editor at the Hugo-nominated Apex Magazine. She is co-editor of the When the Hero Comes Home anthology series with Ed Greenwood. Her short fiction has been a finalist for the Parsec award, and has appeared in anthologies including *Carbide Tipped Pens* from Tor. Her first novel, set in the Pathfinder RPG world, is forthcoming in 2016 from Paizo. For more information, visit gabrielle-edits.com.

Julie Kagawa

Julie Kagawa is the internationally bestselling author of The Iron Fey series, the Blood of Eden trilogy, and The Talon Saga. Born in Sacramento, she has been a bookseller and an animal trainer, and enjoys reading, painting, sculpting miniature dragons from clay, playing in her garden and training in martial arts. She lives near Louisville, Kentucky, with her husband and a plethora of pets. Visit her at www. JulieKagawa.com.

Adrienne Kress

Adrienne Kress is a Toronto born actor and author who loves to play make-believe. She also loves hot chocolate. And cheese. Not necessarily together. She is the author of two children's novels: *Alex and the Ironic Gentleman* and *Timothy and the Dragon's Gate* (Scholastic) and is a theatre graduate of the Univeristy of Toronto and London Academy of Music and Dramatic Arts in the UK. Published around the world, *Alex* was featured in the New York Post as a "Post Potter Pick," as well as on the CBS early show. It won the Heart of Hawick Children's Book Award in the UK and was nominated for the Red Cedar. The sequel, *Timothy*, was nominated for the Audie, Red Cedar and Manitoba Young Readers Choice Awards, and was recently optioned for film.

Sassafras Lowrey

Sassafras Lowrey got hir start writing as a punk zinester in Portland, Oregon. Ze is the editor of the two-time American Library Association honored & Lambda Literary Finalist *Kicked Out* anthology, and *Leather Ever After*, a Finalist for the National Leather Association Writing Award. Sassafras' debut novel *Roving Pack* (www.RovingPack.com) was honored by the American Library Association and chronicles the underground lives of gender-radical queer youth searching for identity, community and belonging. Sassafras is the

2013 winner of the Lambda Literary Foundation's Berzon Emerging Writer Award. Ze lives and writes in Brooklyn with hir partner, two dogs of dramatically different sizes, two bossy cats, and a kitten. Learn more at www.SassafrasLowrey.com.

Laurie McLean

Laurie McLean spent 20 years as the CEO of a PR agency and 8 years as an agent/senior agent at Larsen Pomada Literary Agents before forming Fuse Literary in 2013 with her two partners. At Fuse, Laurie specializes in adult genre fiction plus middle-grade and young adult children's books. She prefers to receive the first ten pages and a 1-2 page plot synopsis of a completed/polished manuscript via email (no attachments, please...cut and paste your submission into the body of your email query) at: querylaurie@fuseliterary.com. For more on Laurie, check out her blog at agentsavant.com, follow her on Twitter @agentsavant, and visit her Facebook page. Prior to founding Foreword, Laurie was also the Dean of San Francisco Writers University and on the management team of the San Francisco Writers Conference.

E.C. Myers

E.C. Myers is the author of the novels *Fair Coin* (recipient of the 2012 Andre Norton Award), *Quantum Coin*, and *The Silence of Six*. His short stories have appeared in anthologies and magazines including *Kaleidoscope: Diverse YA Science Fiction and Fantasy Stories*. You can find traces of him all over the Internet, but especially at http://ecmyers.net and on Twitter as @ecmyers.

Leah Petersen

Leah Petersen lives in North Carolina, manipulating numbers by day and the universe by night. She prides herself on being able to hold a book with her feet so she can knit while reading. She's still working on knitting while writing. Her debut science fiction trilogy, the Physics of Falling series (*Fighting Gravity, Cascade Effect, Impact Velocity*) is available from Dragon Moon Press. You can find Leah online at leahpetersen.com, on Twitter (@LeahPetersen), and at Facebook.com/LeahPetersenAuthor.

Allen Steele

Allen Steele is the author of nineteen SF novels, including the critically-acclaimed *Apollo's Outcasts*. His novels and stories have been reprinted worldwide and have received three Hugo awards, and he is also the recipient of the Robert A. Heinlein Award. He lives in western Massachusetts with his wife and dogs, and is currently at work on his next young adult novel.

Pam van Hylckama Vlieg

Pam van Hylckama Vlieg started Bookalicious in 2008, thinking that a book blog was quite the unique endeavor. She was wrong. Now Pam's blog is one of the largest kid-lit blogs on the interwebs and she has a myriad of reviewers helping her get the word out about books. She is also a literary agent at D4EO, which seemed like the natural next step on her book advocation world domination tour. She can be found online at Bookalicious.org, @BookaliciousPam, and Bookalicious. Tumblr.com.